Aura's Journey

Aura's Journey

God's Faithfulness in the Life of a Young Honduran Deaf Woman

Barbara E. Northup

2011

WHAT READERS ARE SAYING ABOUT AURA'S JOURNEY

DR. DENNIS RAINEY
FamilyLife Ministries, CEO

A compelling story of a little girl's courageous faith, one family's tenacious love, and the providence of Almighty God. *Aura's Journey* is filled with twists and turns of how God takes our deepest wounds and uses them for His purposes. What a great story of redemption and hope! I read it cover to cover and never put it down.

DR. SHERRY SHAW
Associate Professor, Program Director of ASL/English Interpreting, University of North Florida

Aura's Journey is the amazing tale of how lives are changed when hearts are receptive to the voice of an awesome God. It is the story of love and grace, told by a masterful writer who reveals a miraculous intersection of divergent worlds where God reigns. The fabric of Aura's story is woven with a warmth and sensitivity that awakens a sense of purpose during times in which we may feel useless. We learn from this encounter with Aura, the Northup family, and all those who surround them that God is always at work in our midst. Experiencing *Aura's Journey* through the eyes of such diverse characters is a guarantee that the person you are when you start reading it will not be the person you are afterwards.

CHRISTY OWEN
Executive Director of New Life Deaf Ministry, Tegucigalpa, Honduras

If you've ever thought to yourself, "I can't really make a difference.", this book is for you. *Aura's Journey* shows how God can take all of our weaknesses, doubts, fears, and even disabilities and turn the ordinary water of our lives into wine for His glory. This is a book about everyday faith and perseverance through the beautiful story of one little Deaf Honduran girl's life.

STACEY HAMMONS
Fellowship Bible Church, Women's Ministry Pastor

Aura's Journey is a story I will never forget. Walking through this tale of helplessness turned hopefulness was inspirational to me on many levels. I learned so much about the deaf community, but even more so about God's community, and how He weaves His story through different lives, families and countries. I highly recommend this book!

REV. BOB SLAGLEY
Antioch Missionary Baptist Deaf Church,
Pastor/New Life Deaf Ministry Board Member

Aura's Journey is a reminder of how Great our God is and what He can do in the lives of people the world might have considered as having no hope. It is truly God's story because none of us could have written the script for Aura's life from her tiny village in Honduras. The spark was from God and the opportunities He presented in the lives of the people He used and from Aura's faith. Her personal journey of faith is remarkable and is a testimony to the Love and the Power of God toward His children.

BILL PARKINSON
Fellowship Bible Church, SageWorks Pastor

With the authenticity and wonder of an eyewitness to the miraculous, Barbara Northup's book, *Aura's Journey*, pulls back the curtain and gives us a glimpse of God sovereignly working in our lives to both bless us and accomplish His eternal purposes. As the years of this beautiful girl's life unfold, we realize that while each of our lives is a unique story, it is also an integral part of the greater story of God's mercy and grace. In the end, Aura's journey challenges us to trust God every day and in so doing, powerfully proclaim His salvation through our own special and often mysterious journey.

PAT RITTENHOUSE
Teacher, Tennessee School for the Deaf;
New Life Deaf Ministry Board Member

Aura's Journey crossed paths with my own. My family has witnessed first-hand the blessings that resulted from the Northups opening their hearts and home to this beautiful Honduran girl. In turn, the blessings flowed to the community surrounding them. Our lives were impacted by Aura, as we chose to visit her home country as short-term missionaries and met our future adoptive daughter there; and consequently became involved in New Life Deaf Ministry, which Aura serves today. If you ever wondered whether events in your life are the result of coincidences or divine opportunities, you should read this story. You'd wonder no more.

FIRST PRINTING
December 2011

ISBN-13: 978-0-615-56733-4

Editing by
Dr. Lynda Wilson

Cover design and formatting by
Jenny Yancey

Scripture quotations are from the New International Version of the Holy Bible.

Cover and graduation photographs copyrighted by Lifetouch Portrait Studios.

Song lyrics for "No Less Than Faithful" written by Don Pardoe and Joel Lindsey.
Copyright 1992 LITA (ASCAP) & N.B. Music (ASCAP)

PRINTED IN THE UNITED STATES OF AMERICA
Printed by

TARGET PRINTING COMPANY, INC.
1907 Appianway • Little Rock, Arkansas 72204

To my mom and grandmother (Mam)
who lived lives of unquestionable belief
in God's faithfulness

ACKNOWLEDGEMENTS

I would like to express my heartfelt appreciation to all those whose encouragement and support made *Aura's Journey* a reality.

I am incredibly humbled to be surrounded by a family who lives outside of themselves. Thank you, Ernie, Jennifer, Karen, Sarah Beth and Katie for listening to me constantly think out loud about *Aura's Journey*, helping with all the details of reading, preliminary editing and formatting, and encouraging me every step of the way. I am indeed blessed beyond measure.

A book is not just about the author's work but rather a team effort. I am so grateful for two people whose heartfelt labor helped to bring *Aura's Journey* to fruition. Dr. Lynda Wilson is a gifted editor. Lynda, you have also become a dear friend and kindred spirit. Jenny Yancey is a gifted artist/designer and formatter. How touched I am, Jenny, by your tender heart for this story and your labor of love.

Aura's Journey was lifted up in prayer by many individuals. I thank all of you who prayed through the process. I especially am grateful for my sweet 93 year-old friend, Miz Kitty, a prayer warrior, who fervently prayed for God's guidance in the writing and dissemination of this book. Thank you for always saying, "May those who read *Aura's Journey* feel the hem of His garment in every word."

"One hundred years from now it will not matter what my bank account was, the sort of house I lived in, or the kind of car

I drove...but the world may be different because I was important in the life of a child." This quote by Forest E. Witcraft perfectly describes the administration and staff of the Arkansas School for the Deaf during Aura's years there. You invested your talents, time and love into Aura as well as all your students, and our family is forever thankful.

I feel indebted to the numerous friends who read *Aura's Journey* in its early stages and responded, lifted me up in times of doubt, and gave me much needed advice and guidance. You know who you are, but I am not sure you know how much I love each of you and appreciate your feedback and friendship.

INTRODUCTION

Never would I have expected anything out of the ordinary to have happened to me. For most of my years, life has been quite average. Avoiding risk-taking behaviors has always been my forte. No bungee jumping, climbing up the side of a mountain, or exploring a dark, damp cave for me. I don't even ride roller coasters at the fair.

The small rural town in which I grew up was also ordinary. The population was approximately 800 people. Streets were canopied with large elm and oak trees, and houses were quaint with doors that were never locked. The only entertainment for teens was to drive around the Root Beer Stand on a Saturday night honking at friends. Thirty-three students were in my graduation class, and our school mascot was a catfish. Yes, that's right – catfish!

A facet of my life that was not so ordinary was being the child of deaf parents. Dad, who had some residual hearing wore a 1950s hearing aid with a long, thin cord that plugged into a receiver under his T-shirt. He was the town barber and communicated with signs and speech. Mom was profoundly deaf and communicated totally in sign language. Though she heard nothing from birth, I swear that woman could feel the vibration of a pin drop. She was a stay-at-home mom who washed every Monday and ironed everything from pillow cases to Dad's underwear. It was definitely small town America in the 1950s.

With the exception of having deaf parents, it was a childhood that has been experienced by thousands of today's Baby Boomers.

Role models for me were always just ordinary people, church-goers with strong faith. They were educated, hard-working individuals who had an unwavering belief in a sovereign, yet personal God. Scripture verses were given to me in Sunday School and Girls' Auxiliary that spoke of God's plan and purpose for each of us. Throughout my life, this paradigm of faith in an up-close and personal God became my worldview; a belief that was not simply a religion, but rather a relationship.

Perhaps this is why whenever a door opened for me in my education or career, I knew it was God's hand that turned the knob. When people came into my life who either blessed me tremendously or I had the privilege to bless, it was God who led them there. If I was in a hard place in my life, it was God's love and mercy that brought me through. Repeatedly, God's presence has been real to me. But, He has never been more real, nor have I ever seen His mighty hand at work more, than in the story I am about to relate. It is not a story about seeing a divine billboard written just for me by the finger of God. Nor did I ever hear God's voice audibly speaking to me. Yet, as the story quietly and assuredly unfolded, this small town, non-risk taker had to learn to step out in real faith and watch as God took the ordinary and did something extraordinary indeed.

AURA'S
JOURNEY

I have called you by name,
and you are mine.

ISAIAH 43:1b

CHAPTER 1

It was mid-July, 1991 in a small country village outside the capital city of Honduras, Central America. Inside a small, make-shift dental clinic, a Honduran dentist, Yami, and an American medical mission team worked non-stop treating Honduran children and adults. The air was heavy with a stench of dirt and sweat. Sparse furnishings lined the wall; a tattered dental chair beckoned scared children to come and sit. Worn, wooden benches welcomed some of the poorest people on God's earth to receive long-awaited dental care.

Suddenly, the door opened and in walked a precious little girl, clinging tightly to her aunt's hand. The aunt spoke softly to Yami and was told to take a seat on one of the benches. Wide-eyed and curious, the little girl sat down and wondered what was about to happen.

For this little girl, the day had begun like any other. She ate a meager tortilla for breakfast, helped to sweep their home's dirt floor, then rode on an overcrowded bus from her little mud shack to an area near the capital city of Tegucigalpa. Now, the little girl sat and quietly observed her surroundings. Parents, children and workers were moving their mouths in conversation, but her world was always silent. She had no idea what they were saying. Children were talking to her, but she had no way to respond. In her eleven years of life, language was still locked inside of her. However, in just a few hours, this day would forever change her life and put her on a journey that no one would have imagined possible.

Only a few weeks later and approximately 1500 miles away in another capital city, Little Rock, Arkansas, the day also began normally for the Northup family. Inside a comfortably furnished, two-story brick air-conditioned home, the morning rush was set in motion. A nutritious, filling breakfast was being prepared; brown paper bag lunches with notes from Mom were set out for the children; and, the routine of traveling to school and work in modern air-conditioned cars was about to start. Morning conversation about the day's plans filled the rooms. Daughters talked, giggled and argued with each other and Mom in an auditory language while conversing with Dad in a visual language. Mouths were moving and hands were flying as each one communicated easily and without hesitation. We were unaware that in only a few hours, our lives would begin an unbelievable, life-altering journey.

My husband, Ernie, who is deaf, works in the Accounting Office of United Parcel Service. I am the Communication Specialist at the Arkansas School for the Deaf (ASD) – a place that has deep roots for me. My parents, uncles, and Ernie graduated from there. Ernie and I have four wonderful daughters: Jennifer – 18; Karen – 15; Sarah Beth – 10; and Katie – 8. We are like millions of other working middle-class American families – trying to provide what is best for our girls, surviving the daily struggles and stresses of life, and doing our best to live out our Christian faith. However, life has a way of suddenly changing. What's more, God has a way of coming along side each of us and saying, "I have a challenge for you, and I want you to take it on."

That challenge did indeed come. It was early September, and Arkansas was experiencing a particularly warm autumn. As a working wife and mother, I had a morning routine that seldom varied. I prepared breakfast, bagged lunches, kissed Ernie goodbye, chauffeured two of the girls to school, then hurriedly headed to work. Soon the scenic beauty of the Arkansas School for the Deaf campus came into view. Older buildings atop a gently rolling hill with the State Capitol in the foreground and the lazy-flowing Arkansas River in the background always tendered my heart. Driving under the arch that read "Arkansas School for the Deaf," I felt grateful that I could work in a place that meant so much to me. My grandmother had helped establish the first PTA there in the mid-1930s; my three uncles and my mom walked this very campus throughout their academic years, and my sweet husband also spent all his school years on this campus. It was not just a place of education for them; it was their home, a place where they learned their worth as Deaf Americans and their values in life. And, now it was my turn to carry on a legacy of love and devotion to the education of children who were deaf and hard of hearing.

Finally, I arrived at my office to begin my day. Paperwork was stacked high on my desk, which reminded me that there would be no walks from building to building to check on the sign language needs for the day. The goal was to complete paperwork, and that is exactly what I set out to do. Time passed quickly, and suddenly it was noon. A colleague of mine yelled from another office, "Barbara, we're going to lunch. Wanna join us?" I seldom pass up an opportunity to have lunch off campus with friends, but I knew my willpower needed to prevail, so I dutifully declined. "You go ahead," I replied, "I'll stay and answer the phones." They left, and I busied myself with work, praying that the phone would not ring too often. I believe strongly in the power of prayer, but this time God did not see fit to stifle the phone. There it was – line one flashing and ringing.

I was tempted to let it ring – after all it was lunch time – but my conscience prevailed, so I pleasantly answered "Arkansas School for the Deaf – Student Services. Barbara here. How may I help you?" At the other end was a deep, friendly male voice. "Uh… yes, hello. My name is John Pate. You don't know me, and I don't know anything about deafness, but I desperately need to talk with someone about a little deaf girl I met in Honduras." Hearing the words, "a little deaf girl," I was immediately intrigued.

As John explained his situation, I became more enthralled with the story. John had been part of the medical mission group who had traveled to Honduras to work on a dental team. While working at the clinic, he met a little girl, accompanied by her aunt, who took her turn on a worn bench. John spoke so tenderly of this little 11-year-old girl who he described as very small, malnourished and looking more like seven or eight years old than eleven. Allen Danforth, the founder and president of World Gospel Outreach (WGO) sponsoring the mission team, was fluent in Spanish and asked the aunt about the little girl's situation. After that talk, the team learned that this precious little girl was born profoundly deaf and in her eleven years had never been to school. She could not read, write or communicate in any way. Because of her deafness, she was isolated and therefore had no formal language – no spoken language, no written language, no visual language. I also learned there were no accredited academic schools for the deaf in Honduras and very little services for deaf children or their families within the public or private sector.

In the quiet of my office, as John was speaking, I felt an instant tugging at my heart. I wanted to see and meet this little girl; I wanted to help free her from being locked inside herself because of the absence of language. John continued to tell me that he had close contacts at Arkansas Children's Hospital. Allen was able to meet with the mother and told her of this. After a long conversation, Allen convinced her to allow them to bring this little girl back to America with the purpose of investigating what services could be provided. Amazingly, the mother agreed. What sacrificial love this mother had for her daughter to give her such an opportunity. John's dilemma was how to communicate with this child on the plane which prompted his call to our school. This little girl would be leaving her family, experiencing her first flight, and stepping into a new country where strangers would greet her. Efforts to communicate with her would be priority. John and I discussed ways in which I could help him. It was decided that he would come to my office and pick up a picture book of children's signs. This would help in easing some communication difficulties that might arise. As we ended our conversation, I asked, "John, when you and Allen arrive here in Little Rock, please bring her to my office. I am so touched by this story and want to meet her!" He promised he would. "John, before we hang up, what is the little girl's name?" I asked. He responded, "Aura."

Aura. What a sweet and simple name. Suddenly, a memory of Dr. Robert Lewis, our lead pastor, teaching about "holy moments" came to me. He explained that there are times in our lives when we feel God's presence in a new and different way. Admittedly at the time, I struggled in understanding what this meant. However, in the quiet of my office, it all made sense. I knew, without doubt, that it was not just by chance I had stayed in the office that day. A plan was in motion, and I felt incredibly humbled to be on the brink of its unfolding. Thousands of miles away God's hand touched a little deaf girl's life and directed her path toward Little Rock, Arkansas. I didn't know why, but I did know that in some glorious way, I was going to be part of it all. Aura, I can't wait to meet you!

Aura

IN HONDURAS
1991

For we are His workmanship,
created in Christ Jesus for good works,
which God has prepared beforehand
that we should walk in them.

———

EPHESIANS 2:10

CHAPTER 2

Anticipation and excitement welled up inside of me as I waited for the day to meet Aura. What would she look like? Would she be frightened in a new country so far away from home? How would I communicate with her? Was it too late for her to learn a formal language and find her path and purpose in life?

In American Sign Language (ASL), the sign used for the concept "at last" or "finally" is always accompanied by the mouth movement of "PAH." Often times, hearing people, who are native signers or have learned sign language as a second language, will actually vocalize PAH to indicate "It has finally happened!" So, PAH - the day finally arrived to meet Aura. Allen Danforth informed me that he would be the one responsible for Aura and would bring her onto the campus. Allen, and his wife Dona, had adopted three Honduran children and felt Aura would feel more comfortable if she lived with them during this transition time.

At approximately 10 a.m. on a Thursday morning, in walked one of the most beautiful little girls I had ever seen. Allen looked at me and said, "Barbara, I would like for you to meet Aura Waleska Diaz." What a big name for such a little girl. Isn't it interesting that the word "aura" in our language means "a distinctive but intangible quality that seems to surround a person or thing." This little girl indeed had a distinctive quality that surrounded her. Her coffee-colored complexion was beautiful, and her big brown eyes were soaking in everything around her. Instantly, I was captivated. It was obvious that clothing had been given to her because she was dressed flawlessly from head to toe. Her crisp white blouse and red and navy blue plaid skirt fit her tiny body perfectly. White knee socks and shiny patent leather Baby Janes completed the outfit. And, oh that black hair. I had never seen so much hair on a little girl's head in my life. It was not only her appearance that intrigued me. Her eyes seemed to be the windows to her spirit. They were bright and curious and, most surprisingly of all, not frightened. There was a certain quality that surrounded her that could not be touched but was somehow felt. It was Aura's aura.

Instantly, I felt a tremendous connection with her. "She can't be 11 years old," I thought, "they must be mistaken." Not wanting to overwhelm her, I cautiously smiled and gestured toward the office on the left and signed "mine." Sweetly returning a smile, she nodded in understanding. She may have been a child without formal language, but she was not without the ability to communicate. As I silently gestured about items around my office - a stuffed toy, a picture of Ernie and the girls, books, and more, Aura was taking it all in. It was obvious to me that she was highly intelligent and would certainly pick up language quickly.

As Aura sat quietly in a large chair that almost swallowed her, Allen and I talked. We discussed the linguistic development of children who are deaf and hard of hearing as well as the options available for her education. Historically, there has always been a great divide between the oral method of educating a deaf child and the philosophy of using sign language along with oral training, if needed. Choosing a communication philosophy is truly one of the most difficult decisions parents of deaf children may ever face. On both sides, they are pulled by professionals who give their own views, and it is so hard to know who to trust. However, when you throw into the mix, a little girl who has missed eleven years of language development, it becomes imperative to make a decision that will quickly bring language and communication.

Understandably, Allen was overwhelmed. John and Allen had taken Aura to the Arkansas Children's Hospital for hearing tests and found out she was profoundly deaf. They were saddened to hear this news. I knew regardless of this diagnosis, her future could still be bright. In addition, Allen had heard about the medical procedure of cochlear implants and thought this particular surgery could magically bring back Aura's hearing and give her instant communication access. As we discussed the reality of this 11 year-old profoundly deaf child, who researchers would say had passed that all important peak of learning, Allen began to comprehend the challenges ahead. After Allen and Aura left, I prayed God would guide him to the perfect decision for Aura's language development and education.Within just a few days, Aura was enrolled in ASD's elementary school program, and her formal education began. People were faithful and God's plan was definitely in motion.

Even though our family stayed in contact with Allen and his family, I never saw or heard from John again. However, just a few weeks ago after 20 years have passed, a friend sent me an incredible e-mail. She had been visiting her grandfather in Northwest Arkansas and had met a man named John Pate. What? Could it be the same John Pate? When he found out she had ties to our family, he sent her some writings he had done regarding one of his mission trips where he met a little deaf girl. My friend sent these on to me, and here are his memories of first meeting Aura:

John wrote:

In the early 1990s, I went on a medical and dental mission trip to Honduras which was sponsored by World Gospel Outreach. Allen Danforth, who I had met at my church, was in the early stages of getting World Gospel Outreach ministry started. I had never been to Honduras or to any other Third World country and wondered what I could do. But Allen assured me that I could serve and be of tremendous help. So, I went!

My assignment was dental assistant. I knew zero about being a dental assistant, but I rated 100% on a good attitude and an eagerness to learn. We began seeing patients, mostly children. One of the days we were there, a woman brought a little girl in to be treated and said something in Spanish to Yami, the Honduran dentist. "What did she say?" I asked. Yami stated that this was the little girl's aunt, and she said her niece was deaf. The aunt would need to stay with her to communicate what the dentist was saying and to help out if she got scared.

Seeing all these little children running around, and knowing that, in this environment, they didn't have much of a chance in life, my thought was that adding deafness made things even more hopeless. Allen was there, and when I got the opportunity, I asked him, "What do you think this little girl's prospects are for a decent future?" He reflected a minute and then said, "She will probably end up a beggar."

It occurred to me that if this little girl had the proper medical care, there might be something that could be done. I said to Allen that it would surely be a blessing if we could take her to the Arkansas Children's Hospital (ACH) in Little Rock to see if they could help her. Allen thought a minute and then said, "That would be very difficult! Taking a Honduran child out of the country by someone other than his or her parent was almost impossible."

In the natural realm, this situation of trying to help the little deaf girl looked hopeless! But as Jesus said, "For human beings, it is impossible, but not for God. All things are possible for God." (Mark 10:27, NAB)

Allen got the names of the little girl's family and visited with the mother. He also said he would talk with some Honduran officials that he knew. I returned to Little Rock and contacted Arkansas Children's Hospital about this situation.

A few weeks later, Allen called and said that the little girl's mother had consented to bringing her to the States. A passport and visa were granted on medical grounds. Shortly after arriving in Little Rock, Allen and I took Aura to Children's Hospital, where the physicians and nurses thoroughly examined her. The doctor came out and told us that Aura was profoundly deaf, and that there was "nothing they could do for her."

However, after visiting the Arkansas School for the Deaf and talking with Barbara Northup, it was decided that Aura would be enrolled at the school to begin evaluations and education. After several months of working with both Honduran and American officials and discussions with Aura's mother, a decision was reached. Aura was to stay at the Arkansas School for the Deaf on a more permanent, longer-term basis.

At this point, it looked like the "Aura project" was going to turn out successfully. I turned my attention to other things, never totally forgetting about Aura; but, instead, committed her to God, and put her situation into the archives of my memory.

Now, it is twenty years later and John finally learns about Aura's story. Aura's journey while in America was indeed a God-led one, and John, along with Allen, was one of many people who allowed God's spirit to move him to action. Individuals stepped forward, not just thinking of what should be done, not just talking of what needed to be done, but rather, doing it.

After formally getting a student visa and enrolling her at ASD, Aura was placed in the 2nd grade with a wonderfully bright class. Even though she was much older, her small size helped her fit in well with the other students. Her classmates Kristin, Mandy, Joshua and Morris loved her. Mr. Horst Wasserman, a dedicated and skilled 2nd grade teacher, immediately took Aura under his wing and tried to satisfy her hunger for learning.

This was no small feat, for her hunger was insatiable. She was like Helen Keller – discovering language for the first time. Mr. Wasserman was her Anne Sullivan.

As mentioned earlier, Aura was living with Allen and his family. His church had given her a large welcoming party where they showered her with new clothes and toys. He and his wife strived to continue her Honduran ties by exposure to their three children. Clearly, Allen and Dona cared very deeply for Aura and were concerned about her welfare while she was in the states. Despite everything they were doing for her, I found myself thinking about communication issues. No one in the Danforth family could sign or communicate with her except through rudimentary gestures. How would she learn language quickly if she were not exposed to language in a home environment? Maintaining her Hispanic culture was very important, but Aura desperately needed to be around native signers where she could begin to unlock the door to communication.

The week following our initial meeting, I saw Allen on the campus and asked if Aura might be allowed to come to our home once or twice a week for dinner. While there, she could play with our girls who were proficient in sign language and meet Ernie who would be an outstanding deaf adult role model for her. He was thrilled with the idea and said he would call soon. Karen, Sarah Beth, and Katie were elated and felt like they were on a new adventure as well. They did not realize how much influence they would have in Aura's life and vice versa.

*Sarah Beth,
Katie & Aura*

1992

Sarah Beth, Karen, Katie & Aura

1992

And God is able to make all grace abound toward you; that you always having all sufficiency in all things may abound to every good work.

II Corinthians 9:8

CHAPTER 3

In this chapter, I am going to leave Aura for a moment and briefly share with you about my own family background. This information will help you to fully comprehend Aura's incredible journey.

My grandparents had six children. The oldest was a boy who was born hearing. A few years later, twin boys were born who were surprisingly profoundly deaf. Within about two years, PAH, a beautiful blond-haired, dimpled-cheeked daughter was born – my mom. She also was born profoundly deaf. Several years passed and another deaf son was born, and then the last baby boy was born hearing.

As the twins became school age, the family moved from rural Northeast Arkansas to Little Rock where the Arkansas School for the Deaf is located. While enrolled at ASD, it was soon learned that all four of the children, my mom and three uncles, were not just profoundly deaf, but had also been born with Retinitis Pigmentosa (RP) – a type of hereditary retinal dystrophy, in which abnormalities of the eye's rods and cones lead to progressive visual loss and most likely blindness. Affected individuals first experience night blindness, followed by reduction of the peripheral visual field, known in lay terms as tunnel vision. Many people with RP do not become legally blind until their 40s or 50s and retain some sight all their life. Others go completely blind, in some cases as early as childhood. Progression of RP is different in each case. Hearing individuals can and do have Retinitis Pigmentosa. However, when RP is coupled with deafness, it is termed Usher Syndrome. Therefore, my mother and three uncles had Usher Syndrome which later led to all four being deaf-blind adults. This syndrome is caused by a recessive gene which must be carried by both parents to affect any children. As mentioned earlier, there is no predictor for when a person with Ushers may lose total sight. Fortunately, Mom and all three of my uncles did not lose complete vision until they were in their early sixties. However, all were legally blind at fairly early ages.

Warning signs that a deaf person may have Usher Syndrome are generally noticed during early adolescence. Common symptoms are difficulty seeing at night (night blindness), tripping over things that are on the floor, or bumping into people, walls, or extending counters. I can still remember, as I was growing up, that Mom could see the stars and moon but would have trouble tracking things due to limited peripheral vision. By the time I was in high school, she was dependent on someone to lead her when she walked. In addition, when looking forward, her inability to see the ground beneath her caused her to walk with a sway.

Some, who have had no associations with people who have physical challenges, may have wondered how Mom, being deaf and legally blind, could have raised a child. I can certainly attest that she was a remarkable woman and a wonderful mother. I learned at a very young age that I had to sign very clearly, tell mom whenever I left her presence, and abide by all her rules no matter if I agreed with them or not. She was watchful, yet not too over-protective. She knew the importance of a child having freedom to wander and play.

An unforgettable experience occurred with Mom when I was about five years old. In our side yard was a rusty red swing set with two swings, teeter totter and a small slide. One day, I climbed up on the side bar wanting to hang by my knees. Somehow, as I was sitting there, I let my bottom slip off the bar and was hanging on for dear life. Terrified of letting go, I began to yell, "Help me! Help me get down!" knowing full well Mom could not hear me. Within a few minutes, Mom came running outside and helped me down. As she comforted me, I remember signing to her, "Mom, how did you know I was out here and in trouble?" She answered, "I was ironing in the bedroom, and someone touched me on the shoulder. When I turned around, no one was there. I knew something must be wrong, so I came to find you." She said it must have been an angel to let her know I needed her. This may sound a little unbelievable, perhaps like one of those holy moments. I can't explain it or comprehend it, but I know this. For Mom, it was simple to explain. God had chosen to alert her and protect me. This incident confirms my belief that God watches over us and cares about our daily lives.

After I graduated from college, Dad passed away, and Mom and I lived together in a small apartment in Paragould, Arkansas where I was teaching school. Her eyesight was worsening. I tried hard to accommodate Mom's communication needs; I would place myself at just the right place from her and position my hands under a table lamp so the light would illuminate my signs. Then, the evening came when the lamp light was not sufficient. Reality gripped both of us. Mom was no longer visually impaired; she was blind.

Mom signed to me, "Barbara, I can't see your signs any longer. Let me come over to the couch and sit beside you. I will put my left hand lightly on your right hand. Perhaps, by touching your hand, I can feel your signs moving, and I will understand you." That is exactly what we tried. After we finished our conversation by touch, Mom excitedly signed, "Oh, thank you, Lord! I can understand Barbara's signs. I am thrilled!" What an amazing woman!

Mom lived independently, as a deaf-blind woman, until she was 87 years old. She continued to wear her thick glasses for light perception while accepting her life of blindness. She attended church with her own interpreter signing the music and sermons in her hands, played Bingo in her retirement complex, and was involved in numerous community and civic organizations. In addition to all of this, I must confess that Mom also did all my ironing. Mom's ironing gene did not make it into my DNA profile, so when she asked me if she could do my ironing to keep herself busy, I agreed. She was pleased and continued ironing on a weekly basis through my single years, then my marriage, adding all my husband's shirts, and all my children's clothing. Serving our family in this quiet and humble way is one of her legacies.

Mom considered her deafness as her identity. She was a proud Deaf American. I will always remember when she was interviewed, during a church service, by one of our pastors, Bill Parkinson. In front of thousands of people, the question was asked, "When you get to heaven, won't you be elated to sing with your voice and hear the music?" In jest, Mom answered him, "Who knows? Perhaps when we all get to heaven, we will be signing the music and communicating with our hands!" When the term "hearing impaired" became the national buzz word, she was not happy. "Impaired" implied something was wrong or broken and needed to be fixed. Mom did not feel impaired in any way.

Most importantly, Mom was a woman of tremendous faith. Facing blindness, when one is hearing, is not easy by any means. However, for a deaf person, it can be devastating. At the age of 65, she had to learn Braille, cook without seeing, and orient her mobility with a cane, which she hated and never mastered. She was often lonely and longed for more communication with her peers. But, her trust in a faithful God prevailed. She took to heart the words in Proverbs 3:5 which say: "Trust in the LORD with all your heart and do not lean on your own understanding." She may not have totally understood Usher Syndrome or why it was happening to her, but she trusted that her life would still have meaning and purpose. A quote from Helen Keller spoke deeply of Mom's life attitude: "Everything has its wonders, even darkness and silence, and I learn whatever state I am in, therein to be content." And, Mom was!

Zelma (Hook) Carter

1916 – 2004

"For I know the plans I have for you,"
declares the Lord, "plans to prosper you
and not to harm you; plans to give you
hope and a future."

JEREMIAH 29:11

CHAPTER 4

The time had come for my family to meet Aura. She had now been in the states only a few weeks. Several days after enrolling her in school, I asked Allen if she could come to our home for dinner to meet Ernie and the girls. The evening was especially memorable.

When Aura entered our home, I introduced her as best I could to Ernie. Remember how small Aura was? Well, Ernie is the "gentle giant" standing about six feet four in his bare feet. Looking up at him with that sweet smile, she won his heart. After all, she was his kindred spirit. Her deafness and struggle to learn language were all too familiar to Ernie. He immediately saw his own personal purpose in this little girl's life. Karen, Sarah Beth and Katie each gave Aura big bear hugs and were eager to finally meet this mystery girl who I kept chattering about. Without hesitation, Ernie and the girls took this little Honduran girl into their hearts and unconditionally loved her.

As we gathered around the table, Ernie signed our blessing. When deaf people pray, it is customary for those around to keep their eyes open and watch the one who is praying. But, on this particular night my eyes were focused on Aura's face. Ernie thanked the Lord for our food, all the blessings He had given our family, and our sweet visitor. I knew this was the first time that Aura had seen anyone pray in this silent language. She was mesmerized, and I was truly touched. After the "amen," she looked at me with a huge smile on her face. Even though she had no idea that Ernie was having a personal conversation with the One who guided her to this very dinner table, I could feel her respect as he prayed.

The meal began. Aura would point at the mustard or ketchup indicating that she needed some. I thought "Okay, Barbara, carpe diem – seize the moment." So, as she asked for each food item, I taught her the sign. She understood. I even added "please" after each request. "Please" is definitely an abstract thought with nothing concrete that she could see, but she appeared to understand. It is routine around our dinner table to sign and talk at the same time so Dad can be included. So mouths were moving and hands were flying. Aura ate hungrily and watched intently. Language was occurring right in front of her – not a spoken language that she may never be able to participate in – but, a language that was definitely accessible to her.

Suddenly, Aura motioned for our attention. We were surprised; all eyes turned to her. She began to gesture about her family. Though it is hard to explain in written form, she acted out many concepts. In her actions and gestures, she told us that the Danforths were not her family. Her family was far away. We nodded because we totally understood her charades. Aura seemed excited that we understood, so she continued. Her hands gestured about her mother and family at home. Intermingled in the gestures were obviously some homemade signs that were used between her and her family, but they were so iconic that we knew what she meant. Her family seemed large, and it would be a long time before we finally figured out who everyone was and how they were related to Aura. This was such a big breakthrough. Her hands were flying, not in a formal language, but in gestures expressing her thoughts, and we actually understood them. The girls felt like they were in the middle of a fun game. Ernie and I knew Aura must come again.

When we took Aura to the Danforth's home that evening,

we explained to Allen what had happened and asked if she could come again. He and Dona were both overjoyed and told us that we could take her at any time. Ernie and I realized that there was something bigger going on here. Even though we didn't know what it was, we were doing what we were supposed to do at the time. That evening we discussed how God must have a plan for Aura and our family. It was another one of those holy moments when we felt God's presence in an unbelievable way.

Aura continued to come over, sometimes two and three times during the week and almost every weekend. Between her deaf friends at school, Mr. Wasserman in the classroom, and our family, her language blossomed and flourished. She was communicating everything that was in her pretty little head. She also was doing amazingly well at school.

One of the most treasured memories I have of this time of growth and language development in Aura was when she was visiting for a weekend. Late one night, after the children had gone to bed, I opened the door of Katie's room to check on her and Aura. Katie was sound asleep, but Aura was lying in her bed moving her hands. She was practicing her fingerspelling (manual alphabet), numbers, and various new signs she had learned that week. She never saw me watching her. Her hands were moving swiftly through the air as she meticulously formed signs to create conceptual meaning. Her language was being perfected. These small, beautiful hands, which had been metaphorically chained because of the lack of language, were now free to express ideas, thoughts and emotions. I was touched beyond words and whispered a prayer of thankfulness that the Lord had given the gift of language to Aura.

But then, several weeks later, something happened that caused us to look at this entire situation from a different perspective. One Saturday afternoon, Aura came over to play with Sarah Beth and Katie. We have a spacious fenced-in backyard, which at that time had a large trampoline. As Ernie and I watched Aura and Sarah Beth walking to the trampoline, something gripped me. It was Aura's gait. I quickly turned to Ernie and said, "Ernie, Aura walks just like Mom. I think she has Usher Syndrome."

It is one thing to have grown up with adults who have Usher Syndrome and quite another to discover that a child may have it. After all, I knew the outcome. I knew the struggles that would ensue, and I knew that it meant impending blindness. As soon as Allen came to pick her up, we shared our concerns. My heart went out to him. Not only did he have to deal with the new world of deafness, but now we had to explain Usher Syndrome. He was shaken and terribly saddened; however, he promised that he would take action. An appointment with an ophthalmologist would be made as soon as possible. He promised to share the results with us.

Within a few weeks, we knew. It was confirmed that Aura did indeed have Usher Syndrome. She was very young for it to be showing up and that could mean that it would cause blindness early in her life. I knew that Aura must spend time with Mom. They had both met and Aura seemed to love her immediately, but now I knew Aura had to see the way Mom lived, her independence and her faith.

From this time on, Mom treated Aura as her own granddaughter. Aura visited Mom in her small apartment and watched as this graceful deaf-blind woman maneuvered from her kitchen to the bedroom to the bathroom without any hesitation. Aura watched as Mom used her hands to measure the very center of her small kitchen table in order to place her centerpiece in just the right place. Mom signed with Aura telling her stories of her school days and about being blind, and then touched Aura's little right hand as Aura would respond back to her. They were kindred spirits. Mom was another person that God was using to help Aura along her way. It was decided that no one would tell Aura about her eyes just yet. We didn't want to keep it from her, yet she needed to know enough language to comprehend what we would explain. Spending so much time with Mom would give her good background for understanding Usher Syndrome. It would also reinforce a more positive outlook as to what people could do even though they were deaf and blind.

Aura was so captivated with Mom that she decided to change her name sign that had been given her so that it would look more like "Mammaw's" name sign. Those of us, deaf or hearing, who are involved in the Deaf community, are given name signs. As a CODA (child of deaf adults), I was given my name Barbara and my name sign at birth. Deaf children, born to hearing parents, who enter the school for the deaf, are typically given their name signs by school personnel. Name signs are our identity, and I would never let someone just arbitrarily change it. Typically, name signs use the first letter of the first name and are placed somewhere on the face, upper body, or in the space in front of the body. The school for the deaf teachers had given Aura the name sign of an "A" moving around her face for the meaning of "aura." But, as soon as the relationship with "Mammaw" developed, Aura decided to change her name sign to emulate Mammaw's. Aura's decision was significant and spoke of the love and respect that were between both of them. Aura was identifying herself with Mammaw in more ways than one.

It is remarkable that a little deaf girl thousands of miles away in a Third World country was guided by the Divine Hand of God to a home in Little Rock, Arkansas. It is not by coincidence that in this home were individuals who were either deaf or children of deaf parents and had experience with Usher Syndrome. It reminds me of the book of Esther in the Old Testament where God's name is never mentioned, yet His finger is on every page. Esther had no idea about the plans for her, but God did. He was behind the scenes orchestrating, not forcing anyone. He was moving and depending on people to step out in faith and just follow His plan. He still does. In Rick Warren's book, *The Purpose Driven Life*, he states, "The purpose of your life is far greater than your own personal fulfillment, your peace of mind, or even your happiness. If you want to know why you were placed on this planet, you must begin with God. You were born by his purpose and for his purpose."

Any doubt I might have had in God's purposes for our lives melted away. As I pondered Aura's journey up to this point, I was awed. In the 1980s there was a popular song which stated "God is watching us from a distance." However, God is not distant; He is involved in our daily lives. Even when we do not know He is there, He is. Whether it is a little girl stuck on a swing or a little girl in Honduras stuck in her life, God is there. Remarkable and humbling, isn't it?

Mammaw & Aura

1993

*In his heart a man
plans his course, but the Lord
determines his steps.*

PROVERBS 16:9

CHAPTER 5

Our family's most favorite time of year is when school closes down for the Christmas holidays, and our lives slow down to a more comfortable pace. Decorations go up, and the large Christmas tree becomes the family project with traditional ornaments saved through the years. It's such a special time, as it is for many families, but this year was especially exciting for us. Even though Aura would spend a wonderful Christmas with the Danforths, she would be coming to our home a few days after Christmas. We were excited to share this holiday time with her.

When Allen brought her over the week after Christmas, his manner was somewhat uneasy, certainly more serious in nature. After Aura became busy with the girls, he asked if he could discuss something with Ernie and me. We thought surely he had news from Honduras that Aura must go back home; we dreaded what he would say. However, as he began to talk, we knew that was not the case. Allen lovingly shared that in the past months, they had come to realize what a special little girl Aura was. He and his family loved her; however they had also quickly become aware that they could not give her what she really needed – communication access to the world around her. Allen told us that the more language Aura was learning, the lonelier she became in their home. We were not surprised. As Allen, Dona and their children sat around the table talking about the activities of the day, Aura was left out.

According to national statistics, approximately 90% of deaf children have hearing parents, many of whom never learn to communicate well with their deaf child. The particular situation Allen was describing is often referred to as the "supper table syndrome." The hearing family of the deaf child talks about social events, jobs, and family around the dinner table. The deaf child never hears it and thus grows up quite uninformed. Allen and Dona were noticing that Aura wanted to come to our home often and was saddened when she returned to theirs.

Ernie and I assured Allen that it was not due to their lack of love or caring, but her desire to be involved and informed. He was extremely sensitive to this and wanted the best for Aura. He then said, "Would you and your family consider allowing Aura to come and live with you? However, it must be with the understanding that she is to return home to Honduras each summer to be with her family." Both Ernie and I looked at each other and smiled. We had already discussed our desire for this to happen and had prayed that it would. Jokingly, we told Allen we would need time to think about it. Ernie and I looked at each other for about three seconds then back to Allen. I said, "Okay, we've thought about it. Of course, we will. We would love to have Aura come and live with us and be our "fifth daughter!"

Plans had to be made quickly. Katie volunteered her room with the twin beds for Aura to share, 11-year-old Sarah Beth promised to be her best friend and sister forever, and even though Karen was a busy teenager, she was excited to have a new sister and promised her support. Jennifer, also was happy that there was a new addition to the family. We were all ready, emotionally, physically, and spiritually to take on the challenge.

So, the beginning of 1992 brought in a new year and a new member to the Northup household. The first few months proved to be very interesting in terms of Ernie's response to Aura as a new deaf daughter. Ernie dearly loves his four girls, but it soon became very obvious that there was a different kind of bond between him and Aura because of their shared deafness. Typically, culturally deaf people do not see themselves as handicapped or disabled. This is the reason that many deaf Americans do not like the term hearing impaired. They much prefer deaf or hard of hearing. In fact, if you were to ask them if they would rather be hearing, many would say "Of course not. Why would I?" That is the reason when a deaf couple has a baby, they are typically not grieved or distraught when that child is deaf.

As previously stated, there are many hearing parents who do not learn to sign or communicate well with their deaf children. Deaf adults understand this because so many of them experienced it. Thus, this situation results in a strong connection and sense of unity between deaf adults and deaf children born into hearing families.

That sense of unity existed between Ernie and Aura, and it formed an immediate bonding. At first it was difficult for the girls to see Dad spoiling Aura in a way they had never experienced. Our girls were very much aware that when Dad said we would do something, we did. When Dad said "no" that is exactly what he meant, and there was no changing his mind. He didn't rule the house with an iron rod, but he did believe in discipline and unspoiled children.

However, the oddest thing would happen when Aura asked for something. Ernie's heart melted. The girls quickly picked up on this; I knew I had to step in before jealousy turned to resentment of Aura. One of our intervention meetings around the kitchen table was called. I explained that I understood how they felt, but that they must remember Aura's situation and how she had lived in Honduras. We discussed how there had never been a Dad in her life. Aura had not had the luxury of having things bought for her or even good food on her plate as she was growing up. Thankfully, the jealously subsided. Soon after, the girls learned how to use the situation at hand to their advantage. Anytime they wanted to do something that they thought Dad would turn down, they just sent Aura in to ask for it. If Aura said,

"Daddy, can we go to TCBY after dinner?" He would respond, "Sure, honey, that's a great idea." As Aura flashed that beautiful smile, the girls could be heard in the background saying, "Yes!"

It didn't take long for Ernie, with a little help from me, to realize that he was not helping the situation by spoiling Aura, deaf or not. So within a month, she was treated just like the other daughters. Aura was settling into the rhythm and expectations of our family life. At school, she was becoming an excellent academic student. Her eyes showed a new sparkle as she continued to grow, learn, and express herself. In fact, she was doing so well in Lower School that the principal decided to move her up two grade levels to be with peers her own age. We were pleased with her educational progress. Her Honduran mother had managed to give her a self-confidence and desire for learning. Now her self-identity as a young deaf person was being birthed.

Our family values a good education and a strong self-identity; however, we believe in a need for strong spiritual roots as well. We wanted Aura to be exposed to that. With open arms, our church, Fellowship Bible Church, welcomed Aura into the children's ministries. Interpreters and people who signed stepped forward to be with her in our Learning Center classes on Sunday morning. Aura soon learned, through discussions at home and her classes at church, that the person Ernie was signing to at the dinner table on her first visit to our home was a personal God who loved her deeply. It became clear to us that Aura had begun to also love Him and talk to Him. However, it is difficult for children who are deaf to grasp some of the concepts of God and Jesus Christ. It would not be until much later that Aura would understand and give her heart to the Lord. God brought another person into her life that would lead her into this decision.

Soon after Aura moved in, we began to find out more about her family in Honduras. People going to Honduras on WGO mission trips would take letters from us to Aura's mom. We wanted to make sure that she knew who we were and that we were caring for her daughter. Aura's mother, Xiomara, was 30 years old with seven children. Most of the children had different fathers. She was basically uneducated and lived in extreme poverty in the small, rural community of Cofradia about 30 miles outside the capital city of Tegucigalpa. Their little mud shack had two rooms. One was the kitchen, and the other was a room in which all of them slept. Dirt floors were swept, and there was no indoor plumbing. It was hard to imagine that Aura came from such poverty. No wonder she wanted to take long, hot baths everyday, put on her cutest clothes, and brush her hair so often. It was probably the first time that her head had not been infested with lice.

Yet, in all of this, her mother had done something right. Aura was well-behaved, confident, and extremely eager to learn. In fact, Katie often complained that Aura was too good, since Katie was the child who often found herself in trouble. As summer approached, Katie let us definitely know that despite Aura's perfection, she would miss her during the summer. Sarah Beth, who had truly become her best friend, was already lamenting that Aura would be going home for the summer and missing all the fun. Karen, our easy-to-cry daughter, did not want to even think about Aura leaving. And, Mammaw emphatically did not want to send her back. She was part of us now. Although we would miss her tremendously during the summer months, we knew that she must go. Aura needed to be with her family.

For the first time, she would greet her family with a knowledge of who they were and a better ability to communicate with them. My prayer was that God would be with this courageous little girl as she flew all the way to Honduras by herself. I knew that I just needed to trust. Trusting felt somewhat like bungee jumping. I needed to have faith and rely on God to take care of her. God brought to mind Mom's verse that she lived by which gave me peace. "Trust in the Lord with all your heart and lean not on your own understanding." (Proverbs 3:5) Okay, Lord, I will. Please take care of her.

*Show me your ways, O Lord; teach
me your paths; guide me in your truth and
teach me for you are God my Savior, and
my hope is in you.*

PSALMS 25:4-7

CHAPTER 6

Summer came all too quickly. It was a bittersweet time for our family. The sweetness in summer months ranks just about as high on the scale as Christmas because, as a school Communication Specialist, I was off work. The sadness, of course, was that Aura was in Honduras. We constantly lifted her up in our prayers throughout the summer. Aura was part of us now and her leaving definitely left a void. This mother bird felt some discomfort with not having all her little birds in their nest.

Aura returned to her family as a different little girl than when she left Honduras. Clearly, she had blossomed during the year. She was well disciplined in her studies. Her side of the room was immaculate with everything in its place, much to Katie's chagrin. Aura was also progressing daily in her expressive language. It seemed impossible that it had only been six months since she had joined our family. We knew her mother would be able to see the difference and, even though the family did not sign, there would be more communication. There was no direct contact with Aura the entire summer, yet we trusted that all was well and we would see her in August.

At the end of summer, we did have word from the Danforths that Aura was fine and not having any difficulties adjusting from one culture to the other. In America, she had daily hot baths, trips to McDonalds, and a toilet that flushed. She was returning to dire poverty in Honduras. What an amazing young girl! She was living out what Paul wrote in Philippians 4:12: "I know what it is to be in need, and I know what it is to have plenty. I have learned the secret of being content in any and every situation, whether well fed or hungry, whether living in plenty or in want."

Finally the day arrived when we excitedly drove to the airport to pick up Aura. I kept wondering if she had changed. Had she forgotten any of her signs? Would she be happy to be back in America or sad to leave her home in Honduras? Would they ever finish unloading the luggage off the plane? PAH! She was walking off the small plane onto the landing and up the stairs. Oh, she had lost weight, and her beautiful long black hair did not have its normal sheen. But, she was here and she still had her "aura."

Eagerly, the girls first took turns hugging her as Ernie and I patiently waited. Finally, Aura turned to us with such a large smile, we knew she was back at her second home. Tearfully, I embraced her. I smelled the strong odor of burning wood on her clothing caused by the open fire cooking inside her little shack. I loved her all the more. A few of her formal signs had been replaced with homemade gestures, but her hands moved constantly all the way home telling us about her family and her summer. Giving every detail, she vividly explained the work she had done, the small cot-like bed where four children slept together, the rainy nights when she had fun dodging the leaks in the homemade thatch roof. She talked about her cold showers outside and helping her mother wash clothes on a rock by the creek. These were not complaints, but rather, Aura was expressing what fun the summer had been. Thank you, Lord, that this young girl had not become so spoiled by our American way of life that she could not adjust to the life from which she came. As I watched Aura sign, I was reminded how much she had advanced in her communication. She indeed was unlocked within herself to express her thoughts, her experiences and her opinions. On our ride home, I felt at peace. Now all the birdies were in their nest.

Our family was to experience many more trips to the airport at summer's end. Each year, Aura would go back to Honduras to be with her family and then return to her home here. At the beginning, it seemed that God's only purpose was to bring a little girl from Honduras here to America for language and an education. However, as our time with Aura progressed, we began to realize that His plan was much larger and more far-reaching than just one little girl. It all began to make sense during the summer of 1993.

School was ending for the summer, and Aura was scheduled to leave in a week. The weekend before her departure, our deck was alive with a graduation party for some of the seniors at ASD. Young people, both hearing and deaf, were having a good time when suddenly the phone rang. I reluctantly rushed to answer it and heard Allen Danforth's voice on the other end. I was uneasy; I instinctively knew something was wrong. Allen's tone was somber as he began, "Barbara, we have just returned from a trip to Honduras where I met with Xiomara, Aura's mother. She has decided not to allow Aura to return to the States. She needs her to stay and work to help bring in money for the family." My heart sank; I felt sick all over. Not now when she was thriving and learning so much. Allen continued, "I believe she may have been influenced by friends and family to have developed mistrust in Americans. If you and Ernie could just travel to Honduras and meet her, I believe she would have a change of heart. She needs to personally see and talk with you." Allen was also concerned that Xiomara might put Aura out on the streets begging, which is not uncommon in Honduras. He was fearful that a beautiful young girl like Aura could easily be in danger of being pulled into prostitution. Surely this mother who sacrificially allowed her daughter to come to the States for an education would not do such a thing. It was unimaginable!

Thanking Allen for calling so promptly, I assured him that

Ernie and I would pray and discuss what we would do. Even though the situation demanded action, I immediately had those old "non risk-taker" fears creep in. I thought of every excuse in the world: "I can't leave the girls and go off to a Third World country, Lord! Even though I've flown many times, you know I am not too crazy about it, – and to Honduras! I can't even speak Spanish. How will I communicate with all the people there? And, money! We are working people who are raising children. There is very little extra money, especially for two plane tickets to Honduras."

Sometimes I wonder what the Lord does when He hears all our excuses for not stepping forward. My guess is that He just smiles lovingly and whispers "Oh, ye of little faith." That's right - me of little faith. That evening, Ernie and I explained everything to the girls and had a family prayer time. I will never forget seeing Aura climb the stairs for bed that night. She stopped midway up the stairs, turned to us and signed, "I guess I will be like Cinderella." At first we thought we had misunderstood her. She repeated it. "I will be like Cinderella. I will work and clean and never get to go anywhere. There will be no one for me to talk with except the mice. Yes, I will be a deaf Cinderella in Honduras."

That confirmed it. We had to go. It's a wondrous thing when we, sometimes as "Doubting Thomases," step out in faith and find God meets us there and clears the way.

Aura left the following week, and Ernie and I busily began to prepare to travel to Honduras. Tickets had to be purchased; they did not come cheaply since we had to leave within a week. Dear friends stepped forward to help financially support our trip. We accepted knowing that God was bringing in different people to experience His blessings in this story. Ernie and I decided to drive to Houston, Texas, and join with a group of youth going on a WGO mission trip. This would cut the costs and also provide people who knew what they were doing. But, a huge problem existed. We did not have passports. Allen assured us that it may be possible, by God's grace, to get quick passports in Houston the day before our flight. Ernie and I are somewhat obsessive-compulsive planners. This whole scenario was totally against our personality grain, but we tried to be flexible and trust. The contact in Houston would be Lynn Clough, an employee of WGO, who would take us to the passport office and take care of our van while we were gone.

Karen, who was nearing 18, promised to take good care of Sarah Beth and Katie in our absence, along with friends who also offered their support. Early on a Thursday morning, Ernie and I said our goodbyes to the girls and began the drive to Houston. Arriving safely, we called Lynn and told him that we were in town and would be waiting for him to pick us up the following morning to get our passports. We knew we needed to arrive early to get in line because time was so critical. Lynn arrived and drove us to a large building where passports were issued. As we stepped off the elevator and entered the room, we were astounded. It was only 8:30 a.m., but it looked as though half of Houston was there. We took our place at the end of one of the long lines and gazed at one hundred plus people in front of us.

Ernie and I began to converse, in sign, of course, about our dilemma and the expectation of meeting Aura's mom. Suddenly, the man in front of us turned around and began a long explanation of how he had taken a sign class in Dallas. Normally, I am proud of people who take sign language classes and am used to people coming up to Ernie and me to talk about signing and deafness, but today I just wasn't receptive. Another man heard us talking and turned around to inform us that he had played on a soccer team with a deaf man who broke his leg and felt no pain. Isn't that interesting? Perhaps it was the deafness?

The room became so crowded that it was literally hard to breathe. Suddenly, an announcement came over the loudspeaker that lines would be moving outside the room. A security guard resembling a Texas ranger took over and organized the lines in a different way. Almost immediately the room felt cooler and fresher. The lady with the microphone continued on stating that everyone must have their beige forms filled out. Yes, we had that. Birth certificates and photos for passports must be shown. Again, we had that. Original airline tickets must also be shown. No exceptions. Originals? We only had copies of our ticket information with us. As I interpreted the announcements for Ernie, panic set in. What were we to do? We must get our passports today. As other people watched Ernie's hands move, they may have thought we were talking to each other, and he was just real sleepy. In reality, he was praying for a modern-day miracle.

Almost as suddenly as Ernie said "Amen." a young attractive woman came walking toward us. She was obviously an employee of the passport office who wanted to check all of our papers. I thought it odd that, among all of the people in the room, she would come up to us. Perhaps it was our signing, looks of anxiety, or the quickest answer to prayer we had ever experienced. Finally, she looked at our faxed airline agenda and said she did not think it would be acceptable. We quickly explained our situation to her. Smiling, she said she would see what could be done but could make no promises.

An hour passed and Ernie and I had barely moved up to the passport window. We had determined that the young lady had forgotten all about us when, suddenly, here she came. Oh, thank you, Father! She said she had talked with one of the passport employees, and he had agreed to accept our faxed itinerary. She instructed us to get out of line and move to the passport window marked "Closed." Many eyes were on us. Both of us feared that people would be very angry, and rightfully so, when we moved up. Miraculously, no one was. As we passed them, they smiled at us and seemed to have a secret understanding of our situation. Within five minutes a young man of foreign descent was behind the window asking for our papers. He worked so quickly that before we realized it, we were both holding up our right hands vowing that all was true. The young lady told us she would walk it through herself, and she did. Within another ten minutes, we had passports. Totally amazed and humbled, we started to leave the building, wondering what had just happened.

Why are we surprised when God handles a situation? Is it because we don't really think He can? As I walked out of that large Houston office building, I was reminded of a line in one of my favorite praise and worship songs: "He is able, more than able; to handle anything that comes our way." Suddenly, all my fears about going to a Third World country, leaving my children, and yes, even flying just disappeared. God was in control and what could we possibly have to fear.

The following morning we took off, on our way to a country we had never visited before and to meet people who may not be so eager to meet us. Overall, the flight was uneventful with the exception of our stop in Belize. Even though, this has nothing to do with Aura, it does have everything to do with deafness. As the pilot landed in Belize, and I let go of the arm of my seat, Ernie informed me that he wanted to get off the plane to take a few pictures. Knowing his long legs needed the stretch, I encouraged him to walk around as well but not to take too long. Eagerly he got up and went on his quick Belize adventure. Approximately ten minutes had passed when I began to hear voices as if people were arguing and screaming at each other. I tried to look out my small window but couldn't see anything at all. Soon, Ernie was coming down the aisle white as a sheet. "Honey, what in the world happened? Are you all right?" I signed. He immediately said he could not talk about it now but would explain everything when we took off. I had never seen him so scared.

As the plane finally lifted up and soared ahead, Ernie began to tell me what had transpired. It seemed that he was taking pictures of the plane without knowing that the planes parked nearby belonged to the military. An officer with a rifle was behind him, yelling at him to stop and move away, but, of course, Ernie could not hear him. The officer then pointed his gun at Ernie. The pilot, thankfully, had heard the commotion and ran down to stop the officer. When Ernie realized what was happening, he was in shock. There have been too many stories in our nation of deaf people being mistakenly shot either by law enforcement or someone else because they did not hear warnings. My six-foot-four, strong and brave husband realized how close he may have come to being killed, and, in all honesty, he was scared to death. The pilot motioned for him to get back on the plane. A yelling match then ensued between the pilot and the officer. This trip was turning out to be more memorable than we had counted on. Once again, God protected.

Our Photos of Tegucigalpa, Honduras

1993

*Commit to the Lord
whatever you do, and your
plans will succeed.*

PROVERBS 16:3

CHAPTER 7

You have never lived until you have landed in Tegucigalpa, Honduras. The airport landing strip is shorter than normal and larger jets must land very quickly and heavy in order to come to a complete stop before running over a cliff. It was a jolt that neither Ernie nor I was expecting, but it was good to have ground underneath us no matter how fast it came. Since that first trip, Ernie has made over 20 mission trips to Honduras and become very used to the landing. I, on the other hand, have never become used to it.

The airport in Tegucigalpa is currently very modern; however, this was not the case in 1993. Our plane had landed quite a distance from the terminal. As we walked toward the older building, many uniformed men, who I could never tell if they were police or military, seemed to be policing the area. Rifles were in their hands, and serious looks were on their faces. Quickly, Ernie and I entered the building and went through the normal check into Third World country procedures. Our suitcases were all opened and checked. Hard-working men in a non air-conditioned facility gave an unpleasant odor to an already crowded building. Thankfully, the WGO mission bus was there to meet us, and we began to make our way to load up. Suddenly, a somewhat seedy-looking man approached us and began gesturing toward the outside gate. There she was. Our precious Aura with her family.

Introductions were brief, but fun. A Spanish interpreter was present to help us understand each other. Xiomara, a very short Honduran woman with cropped black hair and shy eyes, appeared to be excited to meet us. Aura's brothers and sisters were guarded but curious. It turned out that the seedy-looking man was living with Xiomara currently. Even though the meeting was short, I can remember how truly excited and touched I was to finally meet Aura's family. This country and these people were her roots, and she loved them all very much. After visiting for a short time, we all made plans to get together again at a local hotel to discuss Aura's future. Allen had flown back on the plane with us and was there assuring Xiomara that it would be a very positive meeting. We said our quick goodbyes with the knowledge we would meet again in a few days. Watching them leave, I wondered once again how Aura did it. How did she adjust so well to the culture of both countries? I knew she loved both her family in Honduras and our family with all her heart. I assumed that she just realized that each lifestyle and each life was of value no matter the place or the culture. Pretty savvy for a young pre-teen.

This one-week trip was, indeed, a roller coaster ride. We went from feeling like outsiders, not only in the country but also with the mission team that had arrived to work, to feeling like we belonged there. To say this experience was emotional for us does not go deep enough. However, in the midst of confusion and missing our girls, Ernie and I both knew we were where we were supposed to be. Our goal was to meet Aura's mother and convince her that we were good people who could be trusted with Aura's care during her future school years. Sadly, our first attempt at meeting did not happen.

The day and time of the meeting that had been agreed upon at the airport never took place. We were to meet at the Hotel Maya in downtown Tegucigalpa. As Ernie, Allen and I entered the beautiful hotel lobby, I could not believe my eyes. It was like any upscale hotel in America, yet very nearby was extreme poverty. I thought how difficult it would be to enjoy a vacation at this hotel when only a few blocks away people did not have enough to eat or clothing to wear. The three of us waited and waited. Allen assured us that we were on Honduran time and that Xiomara would show up soon. She did not. My active imagination went into overdrive. "Oh no," I thought, "she has met us and decided we were Americans who could not be trusted. She has probably taken Aura away where we will never be able to find her, and we will never see her again." My grandfather's worry genes were struggling with my mother's faith genes. Eventually, faith won out, and I calmed down. Allen assured us that we would drive to Cofradia and meet with Xiomara unexpectedly. That is exactly what we did.

Mid-week, Allen, Ernie and I traveled with a Spanish interpreter to Aura's home out in the country. We left early in the morning, and even though Cofradia is only about 30 miles from the capital city, it took us a good hour and a half to arrive there. The hillside roads were laden with deep ruts capable of taking out a car axle at any given time. Small shacks were spackled along the roadside. Ernie and I saw people living in the worst poverty that we could imagine. We had both grown up in fairly rural areas in lower middle-class families. We had been friends with and seen really poor folks, but nothing like this. As we passed the children playing out in their dirt yards with half-starved animals, I whispered a prayer of thanksgiving for all the blessings we had in America. Prosperity that we so often take for granted.

Aura's home was located at the top of a steep hill which was not drivable. We left our vehicle behind and walked up the incline to this little house. The surroundings were beautiful. Tree laden mountains in the background and various plants indigenous to the country enveloped the small, meager house. In the yard were two of the skinniest pigs I had ever seen. As we came closer, Aura's brothers and sisters excitedly ran out to meet us. They were barefoot and dirty, but I could see beneath all the grime, they were beautiful, sweet children. Even though we had known their names, it was so good to put faces to the names. The oldest daughter was Yaneth, then Daviel, Orlin, Kenny, Jelen, and little Eduardo. As cute as they all were, I was so anxious to see Aura. Suddenly she ran out from the small door of her home. I will always remember how she looked. In contrast to her brothers and sisters, she was very clean with white shorts, no less, and a bright pink T-shirt. Her hair was neatly brushed with pink barrettes holding it back. She looked so out of place, yet she obviously felt at home. Behind her came her mother, Xiomara. Nerves began to grip me, and I prayed, "Oh dear Father, help this meeting go well. Tender Xiomara's heart toward us and help her realize that Aura needs to continue her education in America. Give us the right words to instill a trust in Xiomara for us!"

Ernie immediately went up to Xiomara. He began to sign to her as I voiced in English. In turn, the Spanish interpreter interpreted my words. If the situation had not been so intense, I would have laughed. Six-feet-four Ernie signing to four-feet-ten Xiomara with me voicing for him and an interpreter nearby speaking the language that Xiomara understood. Then, as Xiomara spoke, the process reversed. I think Allen was mesmerized by the tri-lingual communication process.

A tenderness exuded from Ernie as his hands moved explaining to Xiomara his own life as a deaf person in America. From the moment he began, I knew that Xiomara absolutely fell in love with him, and I was not jealous in the least. From what Allen had told us, women, especially in the poverty-stricken areas, were often taken advantage of by men and not treated well. How wonderful it must have been for her to be talked to as an equal and with utmost respect. My opportunity came to talk with her as well. I spoke of my love for Aura and how much our daughters loved her. Xiomara asked me questions about our home and school. I answered as honestly as I could. This was not a woman who was planning to put her daughter out on the streets to beg for money. This was a mother with utmost concerns for her deaf daughter. I respected her for that.

Then, something amazing happened. Remember that Aura's mother had only communicated with her through homemade signs and gestures. This certainly helped and was better than nothing but did not offer deep conversations in a formal language. Unexpectedly, Aura looked at me and signed, "I want you to voice for me. I want to explain to my mother about my feelings about America!" I nodded and began to voice interpret what Aura signed to her mother. The Spanish interpreter quickly geared up for a fast communication mode. (Aura, to this day, signs very fast with a great deal of animation.) Her mother was astonished and tears began to stream down her face. Imagine the emotion of seeing your daughter communicate for the first time. Aura's hands were rapidly moving and explaining about her school and her life in America. She told about her best friends and how they played on the playground each day. She explained her membership in Girl Scouts and all the activities and trips she had taken with her troop. Finally, Aura gave all the details of her school and how much she was learning. She told her mother she wanted to learn more and perhaps become a teacher when she grew up. Aura ended by pleading with Xiomara to allow her to return and continue her education.

By the time Aura finished, all of us were in tears. We were seeing language unlocked and unleashed. Xiomara was beside herself. Allen was astounded at Aura's ability to express herself so well, and the Spanish interpreter had never seen a Honduran deaf person communicate like this. Ernie and I were not surprised. We knew this little girl had waited a long time to be able to communicate her ideas and thoughts to her family. As we watched and I voiced, we were so proud and knew, undoubtedly, that this would be a turning point for both Aura and her family. It was.

Xiomara took Aura in her arms and assured her that she would be going back every year until she graduated. She kept that promise. She also asked that we would send Aura back every summer to be with her Honduran family. We agreed and continued to keep that promise until she graduated.

As we said our goodbyes to Aura that day, I knew a major change had occurred. Her family would look at her differently now. They would not pity her or think her deafness would limit her in any way. For the first time, her family could see Aura's intelligence and potential and realize that God, indeed, had a plan for this young girl.

The trip back on those rutty, dirt roads did not seem so weary. God had been with us every step of the way. Ernie and I were surprised and relieved at how well it had all turned out. Yet, God was not surprised at all. He had gone before us, preparing the way for His plan to be accomplished. At week's end, Ernie and I both left Honduras with peaceful hearts about Aura.

But, Ernie was not at peace with the situation for deaf people in Honduras. He had a great desire to know where other deaf people were and how they were communicating and being educated. Were there any churches for deaf Hondurans? God was still working in us. I could see that Ernie had a new vision and passion. He was definitely feeling God leading in another way. Our first visit to Honduras was ending, but an awesome adventure was just beginning.

Aura, Kenny
& Jelen

1993

Aura's Honduran Home

1993

We are hard pressed on every side,
but not crushed; perplexed, but not in
despair; persecuted, but not abandoned;
struck down, but not destroyed.

II Corinthians 4:8-9

CHAPTER 8

The years with Aura in our home seemed to pass so quickly. She called us Mom and Dad and referred to the girls as her sisters. Autumn, winter and spring she was an integral part of our family. Summers she flew off to Honduras with us missing her terribly. Well-meaning people would often come up to Ernie and me saying, "What a blessing you are to that young girl!" They did not realize that the opposite was true. What a blessing she was to us!

During the fall of 1993, when school was re-starting, Ernie and I felt the time was right to tell Aura about her Usher Syndrome. She was 13 years old and had a command of language to comprehend more than just concrete ideas. It was becoming more evident to us that Aura's eyesight was worsening. We knew she needed to be aware of what was happening to her eyes and what the future might hold. We all needed to hope and pray for the best but prepare for what could occur. Since we had learned that Aura was diagnosed with Usher Syndrome, we had tried to give her a background in deaf-blindness by introducing her to successful individuals in the Little Rock area who were deaf-blind. Several of them had become friends with Aura and shown her that a person could still be very happy and successful despite life's challenges. And, most of all, Aura had come to know and love Mom, her Mammaw, the epitome of someone who gracefully accepted her blindness and lived daily with strength and courage. We had to tell her and be ready to answer any questions she might have.

Ernie and I prayed that God would prepare Aura's heart to hear our words and not be frightened or angry. We prayed that we would be clear and loving in our conversation with her. And, mostly, we prayed that Aura would understand that God did not cause her to have Usher Syndrome, yet He would have a definite plan for her life.

If our kitchen table could talk, what stories it would tell. Not only were there wonderful family meals there, but also lively conversations about every subject. There were activities that involved behavior intervention meetings, vacation planning, board games, school projects, and more that occurred around that kitchen table. The evening when we asked only Aura to come sit at the table to talk was one of the most memorable. She must have wondered why it was only her and if she was in trouble or getting good news.

The conversation began by having Aura tell us what she knew about deaf-blindness and more specifically Usher Syndrome. We talked about our friend, Bapin, who was from India and had come to America to get his education. Even though Bapin did not have Usher Syndrome, he was a deaf-blind man who was an incredible individual. Born deaf to hearing Indian teachers, he was just a young boy when he lost his vision because of detached retinas. Aura remembered the story of how while playing soccer, Bapin was chosen as captain of the team. Angered at the coach's selection, another little boy, who wanted to be team captain, threw dirt and ash into Bapin's eyes. This caused the retinas to detach, and three months later Bapin was totally blind. She knew that, even though he was deaf, he had accepted his blindness. His parents, who valued a good education, sent him to the Perkins School for the Blind in Massachusetts for the last part of his academic years. When it was time for college, Bapin chose Arkansas and was a political science major at the University of

Arkansas at Little Rock with aspirations of becoming the first deaf-blind attorney in America. Aura had seen how wonderfully Bapin maneuvered around the campus, how he used technology and interpreters, and how he excelled as a student. His blindness did not hinder him in any way.

We also talked about Art, who received his college degree from a university in New York and had moved to Little Rock. He became a very successful computer programmer for a well-known business in the area. Art and his parents had Usher Syndrome. We reminded Aura how Art's life was full. He was an excellent employee for his company, and he and his family enjoyed life to its fullest. Even with limited eyesight, Art and his parents traveled extensively. They had taken cruises, climbed mountains, and visited more states than most sighted people. Art was also very involved in state and national organizations for the deaf-blind.

Then, we talked about Mammaw and what Aura had learned from her. I am sure, by this time, Aura was puzzled about what this was all about. As kindly and gently as we could, we then proceeded to tell her that the doctors also found that she had Usher Syndrome. Recently, I talked with Aura about that evening, and this is what she remembered in her own words:

> I do remember that I was 13 years old, and you and Dad called me into the kitchen to talk. We talked about Mammaw and other deaf-blind people and how they were successful, happy people even though they could not hear or see. Then, when you told me that I had Usher Syndrome, I was puzzled at first and did not understand. But, as we all talked about it, I just kept thinking of Mammaw. She had helped me so much, and I loved her. Mammaw was a wonderful woman. She had a family who loved her; she had her own apartment; she was independent, and she loved God and trusted Him. She was deaf and blind, but she did not give up. I just knew and felt that I was going to be okay. I began to understand why I bumped into people so much and why playing basketball was

hard for me. Later on, when I had to drop out of cheerleading and basketball, it was difficult, but I still knew it was all going to be okay and there would be other things I could still do. I was so thankful that I had learned a language so that if and when I lost my vision, I could still "see" my language through my hands, like Mammaw. God was good to bring me to America so I could learn and prepare for what was going to happen in my life. Can you imagine what my life would have been like if I had stayed in Honduras without any language or education? God is so good, and I could never be angry with Him. I knew it was not going to be easy, but I knew that God and my family would help me. I was NOT afraid.

God never promises us an easy life. He does promise that He will take every step with us, and sometimes He will carry us in His arms when it all gets too difficult. Reality tells us that Aura, at the age of 13, may not have really understood what would be happening to her; however, she showed extreme maturity and faith to accept it and move on. Even though Aura joined the basketball team, she realized after a few games that she could not continue. Trying to keep up visually with the basketball was too difficult. However, she became manager of the ASD girls' basketball team. She never missed a game and sat on the bench cheering them on, getting towels and water and using her gift of encouragement for every girl. She couldn't remain on the cheerleading squad after one year because of her inability to see the girls next to her to stay in sync with them on cheers, but she was their best friend and the one they came to for counsel and comfort when things went wrong in their teenage lives. She could not drive due to the fact that her peripheral vision was really limited at her age, but she absolutely loved riding around with her sisters doing their "teen thing." She was not ashamed of her limited peripheral vision and would quickly tell any deaf person, "You have to stand back a little and sign clearly because I have Usher Syndrome."

It wasn't easy, but Aura claimed the promise found in Job 46:1 which states, "God is our refuge and strength, an ever-present help in trouble." I have no doubt that God was pleased, and He blessed her mightily because of her faith. Many times I would go into the school cafeteria to eat lunch and there was Aura with her group of friends at a table. Invariably, if I looked over before they began their meal, they all had their heads slightly bowed watching Aura as she led in a short blessing for the meal. She was fast becoming an irresistible influence in her realm of the world.

I mentioned earlier that one of my most touching memories of Aura was when she was little and I saw her practicing her signing in bed. Language was so new to her at that time, and she was determined to access it as quickly as possible. Now, she had to face the reality that the language she cherished may become more difficult, if not someday, impossible to see. Nevertheless, she moved forward with courage and persistence. There was another night when I went into the girls' room. Aura had moved in with Sarah Beth because they were so close in age and could spend all night talking. I peeked in, the lights were out, but I could hear giggling coming from the bed. Immediately I asked, "Beth, what is going on?" In her respectful, but 'I know what I'm doing' voice, Sarah Beth responded, "We're practicing, Mom, for when Aura goes blind!" Beth was signing in Aura's hand to see if she could understand her. They both knew that the "tactile method" for understanding signs was imperative for a person who was deaf-blind. So once again, Aura was rehearsing for what life would bring. She was bound and determined to face it prepared.

As Aura went through the throes of teenage years, she truly flourished into a beautiful young woman. There were dates, proms, and signing songs on the stage. There were class trips and school projects and club meetings. On the down side, like any teenager, there were frustrations and lessons to learn. One of those times of discipline happened when Aura first joined the basketball team. The situation seems humorous now but certainly didn't then. The coach had requested that, if possible, the girls have a certain kind of tennis shoe in order to play. When we shopped for that particular name brand, the cost was excessive and more than we could afford. We talked with the coach who agreed that another less expensive shoe would be acceptable. When we told Aura that we would not be buying the $100 tennis shoes, she threw a teenage fit. My immediate thoughts were, "Really? This is coming from a girl who up to the age of eleven did not have a pair of good shoes to her name." Aura was not to be consoled. She ran into the bathroom and locked the door. Envision trying to communicate with a deaf child who is behind a locked door! Typically, the only avenue is to slip notes under the door. However, due to Aura's eyesight, she would not notice notes being passed under the door. Fortunately, we found the key. We sternly warned Aura never to do that again and then helped her understand our decision.

In all circumstances, Aura learned to accept wise counsel and become a young woman with strong values. Albeit, sometimes the acceptance came slower. Like my mom, Aura did have challenges dealing with her worsening eyesight; however, all of us learned to lean on our Heavenly Father for strength and direction. Always God was faithful.

Aura

PERFORMING SONG AS CINDERELLA
1998

But blessed is the man who trusts in the Lord, whose confidence is in him.

———

JEREMIAH 17:7

CHAPTER 9

You may have heard the phrase, "God doesn't call the equipped; He equips the called." I suppose that holds true whether you are a poor fisherman, a tax collector or just two middle-class Americans wondering what the next step is to be. Not that I am comparing Ernie and myself to Peter and Matthew (even though, like Peter, I sometimes speak before I think). What I am trying to say is that we did not start out prepared for what was about to happen.

Prior to working as the Communication Specialist at ASD, I had taught in the Interpreter Education Program at the University of Arkansas at Little Rock. While there, one of my responsibilities was to conduct workshops both in and out of state for sign language students and interpreters. After accepting the position at ASD, the UALR program coordinator continued to contract with me to conduct some needed workshops in the region. I creatively found ways to have the girls join me in some of my travels.

In 1992, a trip to a university in Texas was to be the most memorable and have a long-term impact on Aura's journey. Earlier in the year, Sarah Beth had travelled with me to Kansas, so now it was Katie and Aura's turn to accompany me to Texas. I didn't know that God's continuing plan for Aura and the future of deaf Hondurans were waiting for us there.

The workshop was well attended and seemed to meet its objectives. Aura and Katie had a great time playing in another room during the presentations and then mingling with the attendees. During the course of the weekend, we met one of the workshop participants, Christy Owen. She instantly connected with Aura. She was a native Texan and had learned sign language from a deaf friend. Throughout the workshop, I could tell Christy had an innate gift for signing. This was confirmed as I watched her interact with Aura, who also seemed to immediately connect with her. Christy and I began to talk about her future plans and whether or not she wanted to further her education in deafness. I recommended that she check into the graduate program at the National Research and Training Center on Deafness located in Little Rock. At that time, they offered a Master's Degree in Rehabilitation Counseling for the Deaf and Hard of Hearing. Christy seemed excited about that possibility and assured me that she would. We both left that day oblivious to what the future would hold and how our paths would not only cross again but also run parallel on an unbelievable journey. It's incredible how God brings people into our lives and interweaves their lives' purposes with ours.

By the summer of 1993, Christy had moved to Little Rock to begin her graduate studies. Our family began to see her quite often and invited her to share meals with us. Ernie and I both remembered how it felt to be a poor student away from home, and we wanted Christy to feel welcomed. Aura absolutely enjoyed spending time with her. One weekend, when Ernie and I decided to do a get-away trip, we asked Christy if she would mind staying with the girls. She happily agreed. Christy would say she really began to connect with Aura on a heart-to-heart basis on this particular weekend. Christy remembers that they talked all weekend about Aura's family, her time in the States, and her feelings about school and church. After that weekend, Christy began visiting us more, attending our church, and tutoring Aura in reading. We also found out that Christy was fairly fluent in Spanish. She was like another daughter to Ernie and me, and we could see that Aura considered her as another sister. It was no surprise that during the summer of 1994, when Ernie decided to join our church's medical mission team going to Honduras, he asked Christy to consider going as his interpreter. She did, and it changed both of their lives. This is Christy's story of this memorable trip:

I never had a desire to visit any country outside our 50 states. My goals were to finish graduate school, work in the field of deafness, and finally be able to make enough money to support myself. After listening to Aura tell about her life in Honduras, I was curious and wanted to see everything for myself. When Ernie asked me to go, I thought "Absolutely. Why not?"

After arriving in Tegucigalpa and experiencing the landing everyone had talked about, one of the first things Ernie did was to take me to Aura's home in Cofradia. He was right! Nature's scenery was beautiful, but the poverty was heart wrenching. After arriving, Xiomara, Aura's mother, showed me around her little two-room house. I will forever remember standing in the tiny kitchen where firewood filled a make-shift stove and a smoky odor filled the room. Out of curiosity, I asked where the cabinets and food were. Xiomara pointed to a bowl on a table with half an onion in it. That was ALL? Needless to say, I was touched to the core. Prior to leaving the house, Xiomara talked to me about her desire for Aura to know the Lord and to understand about God. I assured her that Aura was attending church weekly and in a wonderful Christian home. But, Xiomara seemed to have an immediate trust in me and made me promise to personally share with Aura about the Lord. I said that I would.

As memorable as this visit to Aura's home was, the most defining moment for both Ernie and I came while driving through the city in a WGO van. Our goal for the day was to pick up some Spanish interpreters to be with us for that day's

64

mission work. Ernie and I were seated at the front of the van with our hands flying about the possibility of meeting deaf people in the city. The van stopped, and a small-statured Honduran man boarded, taking his seat right behind us. As I watched Ernie signing, I could also see this man intently watching our conversation. Finally, he leaned forward and with proficient English, introduced himself as Carlos. Not only did he speak to me, but also he began to sign to Ernie. It was not proficient by any means, but it was signing. Ernie was thrilled, and I was curious. As we conversed, Carlos explained that several months before he had felt a strong "tug on his heart" to seek out and work with deaf people in Honduras. It seems he had been connected with World Gospel Outreach in serving as a Spanish interpreter and in those experiences had met deaf people in the city. We were so taken back. We had just been talking about how to reach deaf people in Honduras, and here is this man who has had the same goals and vision. Amazing, isn't it?

Amazing indeed! God's game plan expands and His team gets bigger. First, John Pate and Allen Danforth, knowing nothing about deafness, meet Aura. Then, Ernie, our girls, Mom and I are brought into the picture to help Aura develop language and communication, grow her talents, and accept her future deaf-blindness. Christy is pulled off the bench of just everyday living to "abundant living" to have a vital part in not only Aura's life but also in the lives of other deaf Hondurans. Now we have a Honduran man that comes out of nowhere, gets on the same bus as Ernie and Christy and just happens to have the same vision for deaf people in Honduras.

As I write these words, I am awed at the sovereignty and personal involvement of God as He moves people into His purposes. Yet, we must all remember that we don't really have to move toward God's purpose. We can use excuses like, "I just don't have the time," "I'm not skilled enough for that." Our favorite is "I want to do that someday, but not now." If we fall into this rationalization trap of not stepping out in faith, what peace and satisfaction we miss. When we actually follow what is unmistakably the Spirit's call, amazing adventures and blessings come our way. Everyone in this story, thus far, just trusted and obeyed, letting God do the leading.

It was an incredible mission trip for both Ernie and Christy. Plans were made to continue contact with Carlos, and all agreed that when another mission trip was made, it would be deaf focused. They would seek out deaf people, where they congregate and how they are educated. Ernie was totally energized about the vision of possibly trying to start a school for the deaf and a church that would be deaf led with the purpose of ministering to any Deaf Honduran who may come through the doors. Both Ernie and Christy returned to the States to resume their daily lives, but with a greater ultimate purpose in mind.

As promised, upon returning Christy set up a time to talk with Aura. They went to TCBY, Aura's favorite. Christy shared her own personal walk with the Lord and "the four spiritual laws." Despite the fact that Aura had been with our family and had discussions about this, she still wanted answers from Christy. That evening, Aura seemed to grasp the concepts fully. Now she understood that just believing there was a God and that Jesus died on the cross was not enough. It was definitely a first step, but there needed to be a commitment of faith in accepting Him as personal Lord and Savior. That evening, Aura did just that. She did not accept Him because we did or because her friends at church did. It was an up-close-and-personal experience for her alone. We were all thrilled with Aura's decision. Another blessing was given through this beautiful young girl. Now, she was not only our Honduran "daughter," but also a sister in Christ as well.

Aura would go on to be an integral part of our church youth group and loved by her 6th grade Learning Center teacher, Dennis Rainey. Many Americans know Dennis as a nationally well-known author and radio host of FamilyLife Today as well as the CEO of FamilyLife Ministries. However, to our family he is known as the former teacher of 6th grade at Fellowship Bible Church who unashamedly held pre-teens accountable for their daily Christian walk. Both Christy and Dennis made a tremendous impact on Aura's teen years. Aura, who continues to stay in contact with Dennis, recalls his leadership:

Mr. Rainey was a wonderful teacher and role model for me. I never had a hearing person, outside of my American family, that would ask me such tough questions. He would talk to me directly and look right at me. He didn't talk to my interpreter; he talked to me. I knew he cared for me like his own family. He involved me in class and loved me. I loved him and still do. The way he taught and the way he lived inspired me to do the same. I did not want to disappoint him or God! Because of Mr. Rainey, Christy, and my American family, I was able to get through the ups and downs of my teen years. I feel I am who I am today because of their influence.

Christy became the pivotal role model in Aura's Christian life as well as a dear friend and mentor. After finishing graduate school, Christy received a job in Disability Support Services at the University of Arkansas at Little Rock. It would not be long until she made a name for herself on the university campus as well as in the Arkansas deaf professional community. Always, Honduras was on Christy's heart. Her passion for the people there was not forgotten.

Several years and four mission trips later, Christy made a decision that changed the direction of her life. In the summer of 1999, Christy began working closely with Carlos and World Gospel Outreach to put together an administrative plan that would focus on deaf Hondurans. The primary emphasis was for the establishment and implementation of New Life Deaf Ministry (NLDM) which would serve Deaf Hondurans spiritually, physically, and educationally. During her work at the university, Christy helped to implement a support system for deaf and hard of hearing college students. These skills aided her in writing the mission statement and vision of NLDM. As I talked with Christy about this time in her life and how Aura had led her into this purpose, she said:

It was a time of great decision for me. When I left Honduras in December, 1998, I came back unsettled as to what to do. The next summer, I returned to Honduras to help WGO prepare for a team that would be coming for a mission trip. I took care of all the finances and administrative duties, and had the recurring feeling that this is exactly what I do on my job at the university. I knew there was a great deal of opportunity in Honduras to use my gifting. After returning to Little Rock on a Saturday, I went to work on a Monday and by 9 a.m. felt strongly that God was calling me to Honduras. The plan seemed clear to me. Meeting and becoming close to Aura, being involved with your family, and having the opportunity to serve short term with Ernie and Carlos in Honduras had all been precursors to what I was supposed to do. That morning I sought out counsel from Dan Jarrell, one of the pastors of Fellowship at that time. I told him I was thinking of taking a year's sabbatical from my job and going to Honduras to help set things up for NLDM. I will never forget what he said, "When you're plowing a field, you don't look back on what you have done; but rather you look forward to what will come. If you're going to move to Honduras, don't look back. If you go, then go with 100% of your heart." Within a week, I resigned my job. Nine weeks later, on October 9, 1999, I got off the plane in Tegucigalpa, not as a visitor but as a new resident.

Sometimes we want to jump in with all fours and rush God's plan. Yet God is not limited by chance. Albert Einstein once said, "God doesn't play dice." He knows exactly what he is doing, even if we don't. His timing is perfect in every aspect of our lives. Sometimes we don't realize this until we look back and say, "I am so glad God did not answer that prayer. Or, that happened exactly when I needed for it to happen." God does indeed equip the called, and sometimes it takes time. For Christy, it was several years before a decision was made.

Christy & Aura

PHOTO TAKEN IN 2011

Be strong and courageous. Do not be afraid or terrified because of them, for the Lord your God goes with you; he will never leave you nor forsake you.

DEUTERONOMY 31:6

CHAPTER 10

During the time that Christy was struggling with her decisions about Honduras, Aura was enjoying the last semester of her junior year. She would soon be a senior; I could not imagine how this was possible. It seemed like only yesterday when she walked into ASD Student Services in her little plaid skirt, white crisp blouse and shiny black Baby Janes. No formal language, no way to communicate with anyone except to gesture, nod and smile. Now, with only one year left, Aura was already looking forward to her senior year and graduation. Then, toward the end of 1998, Aura's life had to take on a new focus.

Hurricane Mitch had raged through Honduras leaving devastation everywhere. During that time, Aura had no contact with her family. National news reports told of mudslides, loss of homes, and injuries. Obviously, this was extremely concerning to Aura since her family lived in a somewhat mountainous area. We tried to reassure her that everything was probably all right, and that news reports were saying there had been no fatalities. However, Aura was unusually anxious and longed to hear from them.

In December, Christy offered to accompany her back to Honduras to visit her family and check on their safety. Plans were quickly made for Aura to leave the country during Christmas break and return in two weeks to complete the last semester of her junior year. For some unexplained reason, I was apprehensive about this trip. Even though this was a pre-September 11th time, it was becoming harder for Aura to be approved for her student visa to come back to the States each year. The American Embassy in Honduras was becoming more rigid. It was a source of concern for our family each time we sent Aura home for the summer. However, seeing how excited and relieved Aura was at knowing she could personally check on her family, I pushed my apprehensions aside and prayed for safe travels.

Aura left, and we received word that she arrived safely and everything was well with her family and friends. For the first time in almost ten years, she would spend Christmas in Honduras with her family, and then travel back to Little Rock to finish her junior year and be with us. This trip seemed no different than ones before until Aura and Christy went to the American Embassy to take care of all the paperwork for leaving the country. The interviewer revoked Aura's student visa and said she could not re-enter the United States. This is what Aura remembers of this time:

When it was time to come back home to America, I remember that Christy and I went to the American Embassy. I was not worried, because I had done this every year for the past nine years. We always had the right paperwork, and it seemed quite easy. For some reason, that I still do not understand, the woman behind the desk told me "No." I thought I had misunderstood Christy's interpreting. "What?" I asked. "But, I have one more year of school to finish! I am a junior at a school for the deaf in America. I must go back there and finish my high school education. I must graduate and get my diploma." She continued to say "No," and I continued to plead "Just one more year, please!" It was determined. I could not go back. As I returned to my home, so sad, I just kept thinking, "What is going to happen to me,

Lord? What about my friends in America? What about my education? What about my future?" I was so focused on the negatives that I forgot what I had been taught: God knew what was going to happen and He was still in control.

How right you were, Aura. When we believe that things are out of control and everything is hopeless, God is still in control. However, He does not expect us to sit on our laurels doing nothing while waiting for a solution to rain down on us. So, while Aura felt helpless in Honduras, we felt empowered to do everything we could to change the mind of the American Embassy.

I have never been too fond of the statement, "It's not what you know, but it's who you know." This adage personified an "easy way to success" which was in direct opposition to my personal values of honest, hard work leading to personal satisfaction. Nonetheless, I must admit, I was very thankful for some of the people I knew in high places who might be able to help make an impossible situation possible.

During my interpreting years, I have had the honor to interpret for several politicians and celebrities. Former President Bill Clinton was one who often asked for my interpreting services at various campaign speeches, presentations, and more. This continued during his years as governor in Arkansas and during his terms as presidency. When his mother passed away, I received a personal request to be the interpreter at her funeral. Not long after that, he sent me a handwritten note stating his appreciation and saying if there was ever anything he could do, just to let him know.

This was the time. Even though I could not get through to the president himself, I left messages and talked with senators, congressmen, and some presidential staff to explain our situation and see if anything could be done. I called the American Embassy in Honduras and talked with a wonderful man who worked there. He was very instrumental in creating empathy for our situation. I don't know what happened or who made the call, but after several months, we got word that Aura's student visa would be extended for her to complete her education. Thank you, Father, for once again bringing the right people in at the right time to continue Your plan.

All of this time, Aura had no idea what was being done on our end. She continued living her life in Honduras, probably wondering what would happen. Then, one Sunday, a deaf man from the city traveled out to Cofradia and told her that she would be flying to America the next day and to be ready. This deaf man was from the new deaf church that had been established by New Life Deaf Ministry. Aura was amazed. She quickly asked him for proof, and he showed her the flight agenda. She packed all her belongings, dirty clothes and all, and traveled with her family and Gabriel to Tegucigalpa. The next day she was flying back to Little Rock, Arkansas, to our family and her treasured friends at ASD.

We were able to keep Aura's return a secret from her classmates until she showed up at the Junior Prom that evening. What a fun time. The ASD staff and Aura's classmates were elated to see her. The ASD administration was so gracious in allowing Aura to catch up on work she had missed so she could complete her junior year requirements. Classmates were thrilled to have her back and helped her in preparing for the senior year to come.

After another trip home the following summer, Aura came back in the fall of 1999 ready to complete her senior year. The theme of the year was definitely one of busy excitement. Spring of 2000 saw us having graduation pictures made, the ordering and sending out of invitations, and planning for college. Finally graduation day arrived. ASD administration, staff, family and friends filled the historic building, Parnell Hall, where the graduation was held. It was a proud day for the Northup family. Aura was graduating with honors and was asked to give a graduation farewell speech. It is my honor to share that speech with you now:

Good morning to you all. Superintendent Dr. Peter Seiler, Board Members, Family and Friends:

It does not seem possible that only nine years ago, I was an 11-year-old deaf girl living in Cofradia, Honduras. I had never been to school; I didn't know how to read or write; I had no language and felt like I didn't know anything. Because of a wonderful missionary, Allen Danforth, who convinced my mother to allow me to come to America, I received a wonderful education. I am so grateful to my mother, a woman who had no education and no opportunity for an education. She sacrificed a great deal for me to come here, and I wish she could be here to see me on this day.

I thank God for putting me in this place to have a home, a school and an environment to learn and grow. During these past nine years, I have loved being a student at ASD. I feel honored to graduate with the class of 2000. I will never forget the memories of my first day when I was put in Mr. Wasserman's class. Remember I had no language, but I had so much motivation to learn. I loved learning. Mr. Wasserman, as well as all of my teachers, have been precious and have taught me so much. I want to thank my wonderful family in Little Rock, the Northup family, for accepting me into their home. I have been their daughter for nine years. and they became my American family. I can be successful in the future because of their help, their support, and their love for me.

I also want to thank my friends. Even though I was from a different country and culture, you accepted me. I love you so much.

As seniors, we will decide what to do after graduation. I also have been trying to decide. At first, I thought I would apply to the National Technical Institute for the Deaf in Rochester New York, but I have strongly felt God has a different plan for me. My dear friend, Christy Owen, is now a missionary in Honduras, and I feel God wants me back home in Honduras. I am sorry that Christy is not here at my graduation, but I thank God for her and bless her for this opportunity. I will be leaving June the 9th with my dad and a missionary. Dad will stay for a week doing mission work, but I will stay for perhaps the rest of my life to work with Christy in New Life Deaf Ministry.

I know that deaf children in Honduras have very minimal educational opportunities. I wish I could bring all the deaf children here to receive the kind of education I have had. I cannot. However, I can go back there and become a teacher. You have given me your best, and I will give them my best there. With God's help, I know I will be successful!

I thank you all so much for giving me this experience in my life that changed my life. God has blessed me by allowing me to be here. Our senior class wants to tell you goodbye, and we will do our best to make you proud of us. Thank you!

As our family watched Aura eloquently sign this speech to the audience, tears streamed down our faces. How humbled we felt. Aura's journey had certainly come a long way, but we knew it was really only beginning.

She was still so young and yet had experienced many travails in her life. Blessings beyond measure were hers, but some had not come easily. Once again the verse from Jeremiah 29:11 comes to mind when thinking about Aura and this time in her life, "For I know the plans I have for you," declares the Lord, "plans to prosper you and not to harm you, plans to give you hope and a future."

Plans. God's plans. What a difficult concept that is for some of us to grasp. Yes, I have to include myself in the "some of us." I am a planner, an obsessive list maker and a goal setter. After all, my career as a teacher and mother lent itself to planning my agenda, along with everyone else's, including Aura's. I envisioned her going to college, doing well academically, meeting a wonderful young man, falling in love, and living right here in west Little

Rock close to our family. She could teach at the School for the Deaf and have a remarkable life. Surely, that would be God's plan, too. It was PERFECT.

However, I realized that God's plans to prosper Aura, giving her a future and a hope did not quite mesh with mine. I will never forget the trip to New York to visit the National Institute for the Deaf campus as a prospective college for Aura. At the same time, we were moving Karen to Rochester to begin her job as a full-time interpreter on the campus. During the trip and the tour of the campus, Ernie and I noticed that Aura was unusually quiet and not herself. After asking her several times if everything was all right, she finally confessed that she was not feeling settled in her spirit about college. Visas were getting harder to be approved, and more than that, she felt God's calling to go back to Honduras to work with deaf people there. Aura admittedly was afraid to tell us that, afraid that we would be sorely disappointed in her. But, we loved her so much and knew God's hand had always been on her, graciously, gently guiding her every step. So who were we to question God's touch on her very spirit. We knew that Aura not only needed to go back, but absolutely must go back to begin this new chapter in her life.

It was the right thing for her to do, but I felt such resistance. Even though I knew it was God's plan, in my own selfish way, I did not want to let her go. Those non-risk taker "cells" began to move around in my brain and worry set in. What would Aura do there? What if her vision became even worse than it is now? How would she make a living? Who would she meet in Honduras that she could marry and would be her equal in communication? Would she again be forced to live in poverty? Those questions and about a hundred others flooded my mind.

Eventually, with much prayer and support from Ernie, I knew I had to "let go and let God." God had taken care of Aura all these years. I had to trust that He would continue to protect and bless her along life's journey. My grandmother used to sing an old hymn to me and said it always gave her comfort in times of trouble. The lyrics were:

> Have faith in God when your pathway is lonely.
> He sees and knows all the way you have trod.
> Never alone are the least of His children.
> Have faith in God. Have faith in God!

> –*Words and Music by* B.B. McKinney

As I watched Aura publicly declare in her graduation speech, her plans to return to Honduras, I knew that she would not be alone. God's spirit was in Aura and would follow her wherever she went. Aura, go in peace and become everything that you are capable of becoming.

It was the right decision for Aura. A tremendous impact has been and is continuing to be made in the lives of Deaf Hondurans because this young woman decided to go back home and serve the One who brought her to us. Our God is faithful.

Aura's Graduation Picture

2000

Have I not commanded you? Be strong and courageous. Do not be terrified; do not be discouraged for the Lord your God will be with you wherever you go.

JOSHUA 1:9

CHAPTER 11

The time had come for Aura to leave. We have all heard the old cliché "It seems like only yesterday when...." It truly did seem like only yesterday when Aura came to live with us. We had watched her grow from a little petite, wide-eyed girl to a beautiful self-confident young woman. Her journey with us seemed to have ended, at least on a daily basis, but was just beginning in so many other ways. I wondered where this path would eventually lead and who else would be influenced by her life.

It goes without saying that the summers of 1999 and 2000 were hard ones for me. After graduating college, Karen took a full-time job as an educational interpreter at the National Institute for the Deaf. After deciding to return to Honduras, Aura left in the summer of 2000. Shortly after Aura left, Ernie and I drove Sarah Beth seventeen hours away to St. Augustine, Florida, where she wanted to major in Deaf Education at Flagler College. Karen would come home for the holidays. Beth would miss home and boyfriend so much, she would be back at the end of the semester to enroll in the University of Arkansas at Little Rock. It would be different for Aura. We were not launching her off to college where she would be home for Thanksgiving, Christmas or spring break. I had no earthly idea when we would see her again. Admittedly, even though I knew she had made the right prayerful decision, my spirit continued to be heavy.

Knowing her decision was God-led did not make it any easier for my heart.

Ernie and I could not have loved her more; the deaf people at our church were so proud of her but at the same time saddened because of her departure. Her sisters were grieved about her leaving. They understood, but they were more than just sisters, they were true friends. We all understood; we all accepted, but, it did not make it any easier to see her fly away that day. However, amidst our sadness was finally a sense of peace. God's plan, which had unfolded in Aura's life, continued opening new chapters and new adventures for her, and He would be with her every step of the way. I just had to believe that and trust.

I would like to say I believed and trusted everyday; however, up to the last minute, my human nature said, "I am not satisfied. I really want to keep her here, Lord, and I know she can serve you right here in Little Rock, Arkansas, close to us." Thankfully, while sharing my feelings with a dear friend, Joy, she reminded me of the verse in Isaiah 41:10: "Do not fear, for I am with you; Do not anxiously look about you, for I am your God. I will strengthen you, surely I will help you, Surely I will uphold you with My righteous right hand." I knew I had to claim that verse and believe it. God would not only strengthen, help and uphold Aura in Honduras, but He would do the same for us.

Many of us, as Christian parents who strongly believe in missions, may hold our own children back from mission fields, both near and far, because of our worry or our desire for something better for them. Let everyone else's child go, but not mine. We teach them from childhood that they need to follow God's will in their lives, and that no matter where they go, God will be with them. However, when they tell us that God is leading them into missions, we do a complete "one eighty" and try to convince ourselves and perhaps them that it couldn't be God's will for their lives. Aura knew it was what she should do at this point in her life. In reality, I knew it as well.

The drive to the airport that day seemed longer than any

of the times before. Ernie would be going with Aura as well as others on his team. The team would be returning within the week; Aura would not. As I hugged her goodbye, I didn't want to let go. "Take care of her, Lord," was my innermost prayer. "You brought her here to prepare her for greater things, now use her and help me to get out of the way." As she and Ernie flew off that day, I knew her journey was about to become exciting and perhaps, at times, even more difficult. God, help me to release her into your divine plan.

Blessedly, it was not long before we saw Aura again. The following year, in June 2001, she was able to come back for a short visit to be one of the bridesmaids in Sarah Beth's wedding. It was a sweet and memorable time. Nevertheless, her place was in Honduras serving the people she loved and the God who had brought her full circle. So, once again, with the joys of a wedding and the sadness of saying goodbye to Aura, our family moved on.

Aura, Jennifer, Sarah Beth, Katie & Karen

JUNE 23, 2001

Life continued to be normal with school, work, family activities, but Aura was never far from our minds. We talked about her, prayed for her and wondered so often what she may be doing. We did not know, at that time, the difficulty Aura would have in adjusting to the deaf community in Honduras and to the prospect of never coming back to live in America again.

Honduras is considered the poorest of all the Central American countries and one of the most impoverished Third World countries. As Ernie and I had seen on prior trips, Tegucigalpa, the capital city, was very westernized in pockets of the city; however, the majority of the Honduran people lived in extreme, dire poverty. One of the most severely affected groups of people is the deaf community. As Christy and Aura began to work with the Honduran deaf community, they found that only about one percent of the deaf children in Honduras graduated from high school. The other ninety-nine percent were left to find their way in extreme poverty by either menial labor, begging on the streets, or being dependent on someone else to care for them. The following facts are given on the New Life Deaf Ministry website homepage (nldm.org):

A deaf child living in Honduras faces many of the same obstacles the country's abandoned street children face:

- Deaf children grow up with little or no education and an extreme lack of communication within their family.
- They may have only very minimal sign language skills and many can not even write their own name.
- Their family often shuns them as uneducable and puts them to work in the home cleaning or taking care of siblings.
- They are not able to function as equal members of society and are looked down upon as weaker and lesser.

Even more devastating than the societal detachment is that many deaf people in Honduras have never "heard" the Gospel of Jesus Christ. In America, churches may offer either separate services for their deaf congregation with pastors for the deaf or interpreted deaf ministries where deaf people join in with the hearing congregation. This was not the case in Honduras. Therefore, how would they ever "hear" or understand the gospel story. They had very little formal language to comprehend, and very few people knew their native Honduran signs to communicate with them. No wonder God had a plan. They were His lost sheep that He was seeking.

Aura didn't have a clue of the statistics listed above or the dire situation for the Honduran deaf community. Arriving in Honduras that first week, she was ready to run her "life's race" with a heart wanting to serve. She had traveled back to Honduras with Ernie's mission team and spent one week serving with them at a school in the middle of Tegucigalpa where there were approximately 120 deaf students. Educational services were given to children who could not go into the public school system due to diverse types of disabilities, and deafness was one of them. With these large numbers of deaf children in one place, lack of sufficiently trained staff to teach, and no ties with the Department of Education, it was no wonder that Honduran deaf adults were undereducated. Ernie and the others, who came back to America, were heavily burdened by what they saw.

This was extremely difficult for Aura. She felt like she had come with a wealth of knowledge that she wanted to share with her own people; yet, this was not what she expected. She had lived as a deaf child in Cofradia, outside of the city limits of Tegucigalpa, so she was quite innocent and unaware of the overall condition of the Honduran deaf population at large. She found it difficult to believe how delayed they were in education. It saddened her that they could not understand her when she signed her American signs. In fact, she was not accepted.

Aura, when compared to other ASL users, was always a

fast signer. We attributed it to the fact that she was making up for lost time. Sign language in Honduras was much slower, very basic and somewhat gestural. Fingerspelling was not used and communication was much more rudimentary. Aura struggled with understanding them, and they struggled with understanding her. Even the most basic of thought and teaching had to be broken down into simple explanations using drawings, gestures/charades, and some Honduran signs that were used by the community. Aura can remember thinking, "Is this all, God? Is there nothing more I can do? I came here to work with deaf people, my people, but it seems impossible!"

Nonetheless, in the midst of these almost insurmountable goals, Christy, Aura, and those who worked beside them claimed Paul's writing in Philippians 4:13: "I can do all things through Christ who gives me strength." It would not be easy, but God never promised easy. He did promise his strength working in and through his followers. Even knowing this, Aura was both burdened and extremely saddened. She thought she would go home to Honduras, be accepted with open arms, and work with deaf people who could communicate with her on a level where understanding would take place. Even though this was far from the case, she knew God had her there for a reason. Her spirit was more determined than ever to serve.

Prior to both Aura and Christy's arrival, Carlos, the Honduran hearing man Ernie and Christy met on the bus, had tried to begin a Sunday gathering with about forty deaf people coming. Carlos was preaching at that time, but many who were coming did not have enough formal language to understand. Moreover, Carlos was not fluent in their Honduran signs. The deaf group did not have language skills high enough to be able to realize concepts, and they were sorely lacking in Bible knowledge. Socially, they were also deficient in problem-solving skills and in working together as a group/team to accomplish goals. They were coming to the church services mainly out of curiosity and as a social event. By 1998, Carlos was gone, and another missionary,

Beverly Chesser, was trying desperately to get some of the deaf people involved in music, but there was no one to teach or lead.

Upon Christy's arrival in the summer of 1999 and Aura's arrival the following year, the big picture was clear. Without doubt, much had to be done on all fronts. Drug and sexual abuse were widespread within the deaf community, as well as stealing due to dire poverty. The majority of deaf Hondurans had little or no skills for success on any other level. They had no jobs, no education, and no place to go for the purpose of growing and learning.

It appeared to be a hopeless situation. How could the Honduran deaf community ever truly understand the love and saving grace of Christ without the ability to understand it in their own language? How could they ever begin a church without abilities to work together and lead? Christy and Aura, like Ernie, had a vision of a deaf-led church where deaf people were empowered to individually grow and lead their deaf community to a knowledge of God and to a better life for themselves. A church that would be not just "FOR" the deaf but "OF" the deaf. A ministry was needed that would meet the spiritual needs of the Honduran deaf community as well as their social, emotional, educational and physical needs.

After serving the week with Ernie's team, Aura moved into the mission house where Christy was serving. She became their cleaning lady to earn her room and board. Christy was not sure exactly where Aura would fit in the ministry, but Aura began to slowly and patiently work in the deaf adult outreach area. She helped to organize music, dramas, and assisted a few of the more educated deaf people on what was hoped to be a deaf leadership team. She also began to handle the church's finances and trained others in that skill.

Here's an example of what Christy and Aura were facing. Christy recalls a meeting with some of the deaf leaders. She asked them a few questions using the Honduran Sign Language that she had learned. She remembers that all of them answered the questions with the sign "I don't know." Christy recalls one particular boy who was fourteen. She wanted to ask him a question that he would definitely know so she signed "What is your name?" His response was "I don't know." This is a picture of the tremendous challenge that was facing them. It required much time and a great deal of patience. Both of these attributes were what Christy and Aura had, along with a healthy dose of determination and persistence. In time, they began to see language improvements and were able to move into drama to explain Biblical concepts through storytelling. However, it became apparent to both Aura and Christy that an eternal impact would never be made in Honduras with deaf individuals until something dramatically changed. And, that something must be education. The idea of starting a school for the deaf, both Christ-centered and accredited through the Department of Education, Honduras' first, was birthed.

By the end of 2002, Manos Felices (Happy Hands School for the Deaf) opened its doors. With five little deaf students being enrolled, the school was ready to begin in February of 2003. Christy decided they must strive for excellence, so only one class would begin the first year, but with the goal of adding a new class each subsequent year. Aura, who up until now, had been Christy's ministry assistant, became the Pre-Kindergarten Bible class teacher. Aura created the Pre-K curriculum for Bible classes which later expanded into a curriculum for Pre-K to 3rd grade. This curriculum is still being used today. The journey continued, and God's purpose for Aura's life was becoming more clear.

First Three (of Five) Students to Enter
Happy Hands School for the Deaf

2003

Aura with 6th Grade Graduation Class
(Four From the Original Class)

2011

Not to us O Lord, not to us, but to your name be all glory because of Your love and faithfulness.

PSALMS 115:11

CHAPTER 12

In an earlier chapter, I had asked the Lord questions about Aura's future in Honduras and how she would ever find a good, Christian man to fall in love with and marry. Like every mom, the hope is in our hearts that our daughters will meet and marry the right one for them. Of course, I felt I knew just the kind of man she needed. She needed someone who was deaf so that communication would be open and with as little effort as possible. She needed someone close to her own intellectual level and also someone who would be empathetic toward her impending blindness. I also believed she needed a young man who was a Christian so that they could be equally yoked in their beliefs and values. Without sounding too cynical, I am not sure that she could have easily found that kind of Prince Charming here in America either, but, I felt it was probably next to impossible in Honduras. It was a concern that surfaced occasionally as I thought about and prayed for Aura.

God knew my concerns, and of course, He had not changed His plans. He was still in the business of gently guiding Aura into His plans and purposes for her life in Honduras. So, despite my questions and my somewhat skepticism, a young man entered Aura's life who was to be perfect for her in every way. He was a Honduran named Larry Rivas.

Larry was born in an even more impoverished environment

and home than Aura. He was born to a hearing father and deaf mother. Larry's family consisted of thirteen children: ten were hearing and Larry and his two brothers were deaf. When Larry was growing up, there were no schools for deaf children. He had received no formal education and communicated with homemade signs and some basic Honduran signs. You can imagine that if I had been there when Aura and he met, I would have probably found a kitchen table and had a little intervention that would have gone something like this: "Well, honey, even though I understand how you feel, and I understand Larry's situation, I would advise against getting serious about this guy. It is important for a couple to be able to communicate well with each other."

As Larry was growing up, he became especially close to his older deaf brother, Jeffrey. They did everything together. One day, after not seeing him for several days, Larry realized that Jeffrey had left home. Larry searched all over the city for him, but to no avail. At last, Larry found his brother in one of the most dangerous parts of Tegucigalpa. Jeffrey had gotten involved with a rough and dangerous Honduran gang. Because of Larry's lack of experience and innocence, Jeffery talked Larry into becoming a member of the gang as well. If he had met Aura during this time in his life, this mom would, with good reason, have said "Not in a million years, Larry Rivas! We would not even let you come close to much less date and fall in love with our sweet Aura."

One night, when Larry was in his mid-teens, a rival gang began to fight their gang. Shots rang out, and even though Larry and Jeffrey could not hear them, they ran, literally and desperately, for their lives. Just as they neared the door of a vacant building, Jeffrey pushed Larry inside and fell on top of him. As Larry struggled to get up, he saw the blood and realized that Jeffrey had been shot. They were finally found by the police, and Jeffrey was rushed to a local hospital. Later, the family found out that a bullet had lodged in Jeffrey's spine.

While at the hospital, a new church group from New

Life Deaf Ministry had heard of the shooting of a young deaf Honduran boy and showed their concern. Visiting Jeffrey in the hospital, they brought him a Bible and using gestures to communicate, tried to explain to Jeffrey and Larry about God's love for them. Jeffrey's spirit was indeed touched, but Larry's was not. Previously, a bad experience with a church had hardened Larry's heart toward a God he did not understand. After leaving the hospital, Jeffrey, who was now confined to a wheelchair, wanted to attend the new church for deaf people. He asked Larry to help him get there, and begrudgingly, Larry agreed. However, Larry only helped Jeffrey arrive and then pushed him home complaining that this was the last place he wanted to be. This mom would have probably said, "That's it, Mr. Larry Rivas. Your unbelieving heart is definitely not a match for Aura's heart of tenderness toward following her Lord and Savior."

Isaiah 55:8 says, "For my thoughts are not your thoughts; neither are your ways my ways, declares the Lord." God truly does look beyond our outer appearances, our weaknesses and our pasts. He sees who He created, and who He knows we can be. There would have been many who God could have said, "You are not deserving of My love," but He didn't. Instead, in His unconditional love, He said, "Through my son, you are worthy."

Paul, the non-believing persecutor of Christians;

Rahab, the prostitute;

David, the adulterer and murderer;

Matthew, the cheating tax collector;

Barbara, a thorn in His crown.

Our God, the "Hound of Heaven," pursued Larry because He had a plan for his life as well as Aura's. The more Larry attended New Life Deaf Ministry Church with Jeffrey, the more he began to experience unconditional love from Christy, Aura, and the deaf group there. They did not give up on him. Neither did his brother. Jeffrey, former gang member, uneducated with very little formal language, talked to Larry about his new faith and how God had changed his life. Larry began to realize how God had protected him in his own life. God loved him and had a plan for him. Larry understood with all his heart that the One who created Him wanted to be His father, and all he had to do was believe. That he did.

Larry became an active member of NLDM Church for the deaf and an integral part of the church's leadership team. Unfortunately, Jeffrey did not live long after his stay in the hospital. God's loving grace and strong Christian brothers and sisters helped Larry through Jeffrey's death. Jeffrey would not be the only one that Larry lost to a gang shooting. Several years later, his younger deaf brother was also killed in a drive-by shooting. He was shot 16 times. Larry remained strong and depended on his Rock and Refuge during these times of trouble and tragedy.

In the midst of all this, Larry and Aura became dear friends, and then much more than that. Finally on September 6, 2003, they became husband and wife. What a blessing. Once again, I endured the landing in Honduras to spend some glorious time with Aura before and during her wedding. As Ernie walked Aura down the aisle of the humble tin-roofed church with open walls, my eyes filled with tears of joy and gratefulness. We knew Larry's past, yet saw firsthand what he had become. His love for Aura and the Lord were evident. It was a beautiful wedding on a radiant day; another event in Aura's journey that would only enhance her life.

Even though Larry had no formal education, he was very intelligent. With the help of Aura and Christy, he was learning to read and write, and was being exposed to a plethora of experiences that he never would have had in his life of poverty before Christ.

Ernie & Aura

2003

Larry & Aura Rivas

2003

God's blessings continued for Aura and Larry the following year when little Carolina was born. A beautiful baby girl who was hearing. I felt a kindred spirit with her immediately. She was not only a Child of Deaf Adults (CODA) but was the child of a deaf-blind mom. God was going to bless her life's journey as well. As she has grown, it has become obvious how bright and gifted she is. She is, of course, skilled in Honduran Sign Language (LESHO), spoken Spanish and English. Thanks to wonderful supporters in America, she is in an excellent private school where she is top of her class. I am a proud "abuela" (or nana). Carolina loves God, loves school, and is proud of her deaf parents. Even though she does not have as much materially as other classmates, she is learning, like her mom, to be content in whatever situation she is in. Larry and Aura are blessed, and so are we.

Larry, Aura & Carolina

2007

These were exciting times for Aura. She was a busy wife, mother and missionary. Aura was teaching full time with Happy Hands School where she was helping to change the lives of young deaf Honduran children. In addition, Aura helped write the curriculum for parent sign classes and spent several hours each Saturday teaching parents how to communicate with their deaf children. Aura had experienced firsthand what it was like to have no communication in the home and wanted the Honduran children to have every opportunity of communication access. She, Larry, Christy and many others not only were making a significant difference; they were, indeed, changing the course of history for deaf Hondurans.

It isn't known what the future holds for Aura and Larry, but it is certain who holds that future. There will unquestionably be times of great joy in Aura's life as she and Larry work side by side in service to others. Moreover, they will both feel much gratitude and encouragement as they experience the personal journey of little Carolina.

However, as in all our lives, there will be trials. Aura will have to face her impending blindness and the incredible adjustment that will come with that. Ministry will, at times, bring challenges and disappointments as well. As we look at Aura's journey, we must never forget the one interwoven theme throughout – God's faithfulness.

He is indeed a Sovereign and personal God who loves us unconditionally. He gently guides us and, if we are willing, places us in just the right place at the right time to live out His purposes. We may end up being on a mission field in another country or in our community where we do life together with other people. Perhaps our journey is to unashamedly live out our values and beliefs in corporate offices, classrooms, hospital corridors, eighteen-wheelers, restaurants where we cook or serve customers, or as stay-at-home moms creating a legacy for the next generation.

One of my most favorite songs is one I heard not too long

ago during a Sunday morning worship service. It was new to me and perhaps may be unfamiliar for some of you. As I listened to it being sung, the words absolutely touched my soul and spoke such truth to me. It made me reflect on the journeys we all take, the miles that we all travel in our lives, and how, if we embrace Him, God is always faithful. Aura was a little girl in a Third World country, and although she had no idea of who God was, He knew her. Before Aura was even born, God had prescribed every detail in her life. His faithfulness was evident not only in Aura but the lives of so many others. When God looks at me, undeserving and on some days clueless to His plans, He is no less than faithful to me. And... to you. Every time I listen to the lyrics of the song below or even sign them, I personalize them. I invite you to read the second verse and chorus to this song and personalize them to your life.

No Less Than Faithful

When the journey of life overwhelms me,
And I'm facing tomorrow alone.
There are times when I don't feel His presence,
And it seems like I'm so far from home.
Then I remember the years and the miles
That once were uncertain to me.
When His grace saw me through every trial,
And His faithfulness taught me to always believe.

Chorus
For He's no less, no less than faithful
Every task in His hands He completes.
At the end of this life, I will look back to see
He's been no less than faithful to me!
No less than faithful to me!

There were many times when Aura must have felt as though she were facing her tomorrows alone. At first, she was miles away from her Honduran home trying to fit into an unknown American society, and then she was miles away from her American home trying to re-acclimate to a culture that had become strange to her. However, at the end of this life, Aura will look back and see that God was no less than faithful to her. My prayer for Aura, her family and friends, for you, dear reader and for all of us is that God continue to guide our every step and that we may know how great is His faithfulness.

The verse at the first of this chapter really sums it all up: "Not to us O Lord, not to us, but to your name be all glory because of Your love and faithfulness." Psalms 115:11.

EPILOGUE
The Rest of the Story

As we are nearing the year 2011, the gentle prompting in Aura, Larry and Christy's spirit continues to move them forward in service. Through the years, New Life Deaf Ministry has experienced the labor of birth, the first growing pains of establishment, and now the anticipation of greater accomplishments. Here is a brief summary of what has occurred in the past ten years in Larry and Aura's work as well as NLDM:

LARRY & AURA

- Aura has continued to fill the role of one of the classroom teachers at Happy Hands. However, due to her worsening vision, she will no longer be teaching full time in 2012. Aura will teach one class of independent living skills to the older children and continue her Saturday morning parent sign language classes.
- Larry currently has a new position with NLDM as special projects assistant. He helps Christy in diverse projects such as mission team logistics, going on field trips with the teams as well as hosting them, and overseeing the maintenance of the building. He is also responsible for ministry cars, plumbing, electrical and works with the construction mission teams.

NEW LIFE DEAF MINISTRY
The School

- In 2002, it was determined that New Life Deaf Ministry would become independent from World Gospel Outreach and continue plans for the establishment of a school for Honduran deaf children.
- During this time period, Christy worked closely with the National University of Honduras. She taught theory classes in interpreting for the deaf and started sign classes taught by deaf Hondurans. While there, God brought a young Honduran woman, Oneyda, into Christy's classes. A soon-to-be graduate in the area of education, she was also proving to have a heart for deaf people and a gift in sign language. She was hired to work with Christy in an administrative role.
- In February, 2003, Manos Felices, Happy Hands School for the Deaf opened. Five little Honduran deaf children were the first students to begin in the Pre-Kindergarten class.
- Each subsequent year, enrollment increased as new classes were added. By 2011, sixty children were enrolled in Pre-Kindergarten through 6th grade. *(See Happy Hands School Chart, page 104)*
- Happy Hands School for the Deaf has been accredited by the Honduran Department of Education and nationally recognized for its excellence in education.

The incredible journey of Happy Hands School for the Deaf is best summed up in the words of one proud dad:

> When my son was born and we found out he was deaf, I was so sad and knew there was no hope for him. Our family would need to take care of him for the rest of his life. When I heard about the school, I couldn't believe it. God must

have seen my tears and heard my prayers. My wife and I immediately went, talked with the staff, and enrolled him. Now, he is in 3rd grade. He loves his school and is doing very well. My wife and I take sign language classes, and we can now communicate with our son. I know he will be able to do and be anything he wants to be in his life. We are blessed!

This is what God had in mind twenty years ago when He gently guided Aura on her journey forward. As I look at the faces of the deaf children in Happy Hands School, I wonder what journeys they will now be able to take. Journeys that would have not been possible except for God's divine intervention. How amazing.

ENROLLMENT GROWTH CHART
Happy Hands School for the Deaf

YEARS CLASSES ADDED	CLASSES ADDED	TOTAL STUDENTS
2003	Pre-Kindergarten	5
2004	Kindergarten	17
2005	Preparatory	24
2006	1st Grade	35
2007	2nd Grade	42
2008	3rd Grade	48
2009	4th Grade	54
2010	5th Grade	56
2011	6th Grade	60
*2012	7th Grade	TBD

* When the new school year begins in February, 2012, a 7th grade class will be added. Five of the 7th grade students are the original five students who began with the school in 2003.

NEW LIFE DEAF MINISTRY
The Church

The church has also experienced growth pains throughout the past ten years. At the onset, attendance was as high as 100 deaf people coming to Sunday morning worship services. Some of them came searching for spiritual satisfaction; others came for all the wrong reasons. Pimps attended to recruit prostitutes; thieves came to scope out the ministry building for the purpose of coming back to steal; and many came because of a deep longing for social activity. However, within a short time, only the ones seeking a better life stayed. Numbers decreased, however, lives being converted and forever changed increased. Here is a brief summary of how the church has grown and changed over the years:

- In 1996, New Life Deaf Ministry Church (NLDMC) was launched. Currently, approximately 60 deaf people are in attendance on a regular basis. Sunday worship services, children's classes, youth group, and Bible studies, all in Honduran Sign Language (LESHO), are offered.
- In 2000, Melvin Lazo, a young Honduran deaf man felt called to become an elder and lay pastor of NLDMC. Melvin and his wife, Wendy, spend many hours reaching out to deaf adults in the community, discipling current church members, and planning activities with the deaf leadership and the church. In 2008, another deaf lay pastor was added. Manuel Chavez, who is an assistant teacher and coach for Happy Hands School, began to preach one Sunday a month.
- As of 2011, NLDMC has made some changes in their church services. The first and third Sunday worship services include signed music both for choir and congregational worship; dramas and preaching. Every second Sunday of the month, a focus is placed on small group Bible study which includes Bible stories, memorization of verses, and practical applications. Fourth Sundays of the month are "Evangelism Sundays" where worship takes place on the local soccer field. Games are played and a message is given.

A LETTER TO
THE READER

Dear Reader:

This story is not just about one little girl; it is about all of us. I have been writing Aura's Journey, off and on, for a long time. The past five years have found me on my own journey facing the challenge of my life: cancer. When I was first diagnosed, I couldn't believe it. Throughout my life, I had been so blessed with good health and abundant energy. After all, I was a "mighty Lake City Catfish," a country girl who could pick cotton and put in long hours of field work with the best of them. I was very seldom sick. In 2006, the phone call came. "Mrs. Northup, I am sorry to inform you that the lump in your breast is malignant, and the bone scans show it has also metastasized on your spine." What? Impossible, Lord! NOT ME.

It was not only possible; it was real. I had breast cancer and a positive test for the HER-2 NEU gene. I soon learned that this gene, which I had never heard of before, would be the reason my breast cancer, even though removed, continued to spread. Over the past few years, the breast cancer progressed to my lymph nodes then spread to my liver and abdomen. I experienced chemo on the lighter side, then chemo on the dark side, with hair loss, diarrhea and low energy. During all of this, I wondered if this stage of life would ever end. Some of you know all too well what I am talking about because this scenario is common for many men and women today. Through it all, when my mind wanders to the "dark side," I focus on Aura's journey. If God could be as involved and real in this little girl's life, He can also be just as involved and real to me on my journey. He has been and continues to be.

I have no idea what journey you are on or where your path is leading. I do not know your background or where you are spiritually in your life. I do know this. If I have learned anything from Aura's story, it is: God created me; He loves me; and He is with me daily to gently guide and strengthen me into His purposes. He wants me to be more like Him and to trust in His faithfulness to do what He has already promised He would do. For me, it is better to live this way than to experience life any other way.

It is my prayer that *Aura's Journey* was a blessing to your life. May God bless you mightily on your journey.

In His love,

Barbara E. Northup

NEW LIFE
DEAF MINISTRY

New Life Deaf Ministry is in the business of changing lives by offering a wide spectrum of services and opportunities that meet the specific spiritual, educational and emotional needs of the Deaf Honduran community.

If you would like to know more about this ministry, there are several avenues for contact:

www.nldm.org

U.S. ADDRESS
General Correspondence/Donations

P.O. Box 55184
Little Rock, AR
72215-5184

HONDURAS ADDRESS
(via Miami, FL)
General Correspondence – Letters Only

TGU 0005
P.O. Box 02-5387
Miami, FL
33102-5387

A portion of the proceeds from the sale of this book will be dedicated to New Life Deaf Ministry.

For book order information or sending testimonials/comments, contact us at: aurasjourney@sbcglobal.net